5G Unlocked

Exploring the Future of Connectivity and Smart Technologies

Alan H. Patrick

PREFACE

Welcome to *"5G Unleashed: The Power, Promise, and Practicality of Next-Generation Connectivity."*

We're standing at the edge of a digital frontier that promises to reshape the way we live, work, and connect — and **5G** is at the heart of this transformation. Whether you're an entrepreneur looking to innovate, a tech enthusiast eager to understand the future, a policymaker shaping strategy, or a curious learner simply exploring what's next, this book was crafted for you.

Why This Book?

The idea for this book came out of a simple yet powerful realization: **5G is more than just faster internet**. It's a foundational technology — a catalyst that unlocks innovations like **autonomous vehicles**, **remote surgeries**, **smart cities**, **immersive entertainment**, and the **Internet of Things (IoT)** at scale. But with so much buzz and technical jargon, many people feel overwhelmed or left out of the conversation.

That's where this book comes in.

I wanted to write a guide that **cuts through the noise** and **breaks down complex concepts** in a clear, engaging, and practical way. A book that doesn't just throw technical specs at you but shows you **how 5G is actually being implemented**, how it's **shaping industries**, and how you can be part of that transformation — whether you're in healthcare, manufacturing, education, finance, or beyond.

A Hands-On Approach to Learning

This book is not just theory. It's grounded in **real-world applications**, **step-by-step walkthroughs**, and **current examples** of 5G in action — all explained using straightforward language. You'll find:

- Real-life scenarios showing **how 5G is transforming industries**
- Case studies of cities, companies, and communities embracing 5G

- Visuals, flowcharts, and structured guides to help you retain and apply what you learn
- A glossary and resource list for continued learning

The tone is **conversational**, because I believe learning should feel more like a meaningful discussion than a lecture. My goal is for you to feel like you're sitting down with a knowledgeable friend who's walking you through the exciting world of 5G, one concept at a time.

What You'll Discover

Across the chapters, you'll explore:

- The **technical foundations** of 5G and how it compares to previous generations
- The role of 5G in enabling technologies like **AI**, **VR/AR**, **robotics**, and **edge computing**
- Sector-specific deep dives: from **healthcare and agriculture** to **transportation and education**
- What lies **beyond 5G**, including a glimpse into **6G** and next-gen innovation
- How 5G is influencing **economic growth**, **policy**, and **global digital inclusion**

A Personal Note

As someone who's watched the digital evolution unfold — from dial-up modems to fiber optics and now 5G — I've always been fascinated by how connectivity shapes humanity. But the shift to 5G isn't just about speed. It's about **possibility**. It's about **empowering people** with access, opportunity, and tools to build smarter, safer, and more sustainable communities.

This book is my way of sharing that vision with you. I hope it equips you with not only knowledge but inspiration — to think differently, to explore what's possible, and to play your own role in building the connected future we're all heading toward.

Let's dive in — the world of 5G awaits.

With curiosity and clarity,
Alan H. Patrick

Table of Contents

Introduction: The Promise of 5G: Revolutionizing Connectivity and Smart Technologies

The world we live in today is deeply connected through technology. From the smartphones in our pockets to the smart devices in our homes, we are more dependent on connectivity than ever before. And now, there's a new revolution on the horizon — 5G.

But what exactly is 5G, and why is it so important? In this book, we're going to explore the promise of 5G and dive deep into its impact on our lives, industries, and the future of technology. If you're someone who's heard about 5G but aren't sure what it really means, or if you're excited to understand the ins and outs of this next-generation connectivity, you've come to the right place.

This chapter will lay the foundation for our journey into the world of 5G. We'll look at how 5G is changing the way we connect, why it's such a big deal, and why understanding it is crucial for anyone who wants to stay ahead in this rapidly evolving world.

Overview of 5G's Impact on Society and Industries

Imagine a world where every device you own is seamlessly connected to the internet, responding to your commands instantly without delays. A world where your smartphone downloads movies in seconds, self-driving cars communicate with each other to avoid accidents, and doctors perform remote surgeries from thousands of miles away, all in real time. Sounds futuristic, right? Well, that future is closer than you think, thanks to 5G.

5G, or fifth-generation wireless technology, is the latest and most advanced iteration of mobile networks. Unlike its predecessors, 5G isn't just about faster internet speeds. It's about creating an entirely new ecosystem of connected devices that work together more efficiently than ever before. Whether you're looking at smart homes, healthcare, transportation, or even entire cities, 5G promises to be the backbone of the next technological revolution.

Here's how it's going to impact society:

- **Speed and Efficiency:** With speeds up to 100 times faster than 4G, 5G will allow users to download large files, stream high-definition videos, and play data-intensive games without any lag. This is more than just a luxury; it will enable industries like entertainment, gaming, and media to evolve in ways we haven't yet imagined.
- **Smarter Cities:** From traffic management to waste collection, 5G will allow cities to become "smart," improving the quality of life for urban dwellers. Imagine real-time traffic updates, connected public transportation systems, and energy-efficient buildings all working together.
- **Revolutionizing Industries:** Healthcare is one of the biggest areas where 5G will make a massive difference. It will enable things like telemedicine, remote surgeries, and real-time patient monitoring, making healthcare more accessible and efficient. In manufacturing, 5G will support robotics and automation, streamlining operations and improving productivity.

The implications of 5G go far beyond just speed — it's about creating new opportunities and changing the way we live, work, and interact with the world around us.

Why This Book Matters: Bridging Knowledge Gaps on 5G

Now that you understand why 5G is so exciting, let's talk about why you're reading this book.

You might have heard a lot about 5G in the media, from endless ads promising faster downloads to stories about self-driving cars and smart cities. But there's a lot more to 5G than what's being talked about in the headlines. That's where this book comes in.

5G is not just another technology upgrade — it's a complete game-changer. However, for most people, there's still a huge knowledge gap when it comes to understanding how 5G works, what it can do, and why it's important. There's no need to feel overwhelmed if you're not yet an expert — this book is designed to take you from the basics to a deep understanding of the technology and its applications, step by step.

In this book, you'll learn:

- **The fundamentals of 5G** — What 5G is, how it works, and what makes it so different from previous generations of wireless networks.
- **Practical implementation** — How to take advantage of 5G, whether you're a consumer looking to upgrade your devices or a small business owner exploring new opportunities.
- **Advanced technical insights** — A deeper look at the architecture and infrastructure behind 5G networks, for those who want to understand the technology at a granular level.
- **Industry-specific applications** — How 5G is transforming healthcare, transportation, manufacturing, and more.

By the time you finish this book, you'll have a solid understanding of 5G's capabilities and be equipped to leverage it in your personal and professional life.

How to Use This Book: From Beginner to Expert

This book is designed to be accessible to everyone, whether you're a complete beginner or someone who already has some knowledge of technology. The structure of the book follows a clear progression, allowing you to build on what you learn as you go.

Here's how to make the most of this book:

1. **Start with the Basics**: If you're new to 5G, begin with the first few chapters. These will cover the fundamental concepts and help you build a solid foundation. You don't need to be a tech expert to understand the basics, and we'll keep things simple.

2. **Gradually Dive Deeper**: As you move through the book, you'll start to explore more complex topics like the architecture of 5G networks, security considerations, and advanced use cases. You don't need to skip ahead; take your time and digest the information in a way that makes sense for you.
3. **Get Practical Insights**: For those who want to know how 5G will directly affect their lives or businesses, we've included practical sections on how to set up and access 5G, as well as what the future holds for industries like healthcare and manufacturing.
4. **Explore Advanced Topics**: If you're already familiar with some of the basics, you might be eager to dive into the technical details. Feel free to jump to the later chapters, where we discuss network architecture, optimization, and security.
5. **Keep Coming Back**: This book isn't just a one-time read. The world of 5G is evolving, and the topics covered here will continue to be relevant as new technologies emerge. Keep it handy as a reference guide whenever you need to brush up on the details.

In this introduction, we've only scratched the surface of what 5G can offer. But now, you have a clear understanding of why 5G matters and how it will revolutionize industries, everyday life, and even entire societies.

As we progress through this book, I'll guide you through the exciting world of 5G, helping you unlock its full potential. From understanding the technology behind it to exploring its applications and future implications, this book will equip you with the knowledge you need to thrive in the 5G-powered world.

Get ready to embark on a journey into the future of connectivity — a future that is already unfolding before our eyes, and one that you're now equipped to understand and navigate.

Welcome to the world of 5G.

Part 1: Understanding 5G – The Basics

Chapter 1: Introduction to 5G

1.1 What is 5G?

The term **5G** often gets thrown around in tech discussions, but what exactly does it mean? How does it work? And more importantly, how will it affect you, whether you're just using a smartphone or you're managing a business looking to adopt cutting-edge technology?

Let's break it down, step by step, in a clear, approachable way. I'll explain the key concepts of 5G in detail, from what it is to how it works, and provide some practical examples to make everything easier to understand.

The Basics: What is 5G?

Simply put, **5G** is the fifth generation of mobile network technology. It's designed to offer faster data speeds, lower latency (the time it takes for data to travel from one point to another), and increased capacity (the ability to handle more devices simultaneously) compared to its predecessor, 4G. This means **5G** isn't just an upgrade to 4G—it's a whole new infrastructure with the potential to transform industries, cities, and our everyday lives.

To understand 5G, let's first compare it to the older technologies:

- **1G**: The first mobile network that allowed for basic voice calls (analog).
- **2G**: Introduced digital data, allowing for SMS (text messages) and better voice quality.
- **3G**: Enabled mobile internet browsing, allowing us to check emails, surf the web, and use early apps.
- **4G**: Brought faster internet, HD video streaming, and supported the rise of services like video calls, mobile gaming, and apps that rely on rich media.

So, **5G** is the next major step forward, and it's poised to take things to a level that was once thought impossible.

Key Features of 5G

1. Speed: 100x Faster Than 4G

One of the most noticeable improvements with 5G is **speed**. With 5G, you can expect speeds of up to **10 Gbps (gigabits per second)** in ideal conditions. This is up to **100 times faster** than 4G, and it means downloading a full-length HD movie that used to take minutes can now happen in just a few seconds. For instance, imagine downloading a 3 GB file in less than 3 seconds!

For a real-life example, imagine you're at a crowded stadium trying to download the latest game highlights. With 4G, it might take several minutes or, worse, the connection could drop due to network congestion. On a 5G network, that problem is eliminated, and you can download in real-time, even with thousands of people connected to the same network.

2. Low Latency: Instantaneous Communication

Another game-changing feature of 5G is **low latency**. Latency refers to the delay between sending and receiving data. On 4G, latency is typically around 30-50 milliseconds, but 5G reduces this to as low as **1 millisecond**.

To put this into perspective: In online gaming, where a fraction of a second can make a huge difference in gameplay, low latency ensures a more responsive experience. Similarly, for things like **remote surgery**, where a doctor could perform an operation from miles away, the low latency of 5G makes it possible to have near-instantaneous control over robotic surgery tools. With 4G, that delay would be too long to ensure precision and safety.

3. Capacity: Handling More Devices

As more devices connect to the internet—whether smartphones, wearables, home appliances, or smart cities—networks become congested, leading to slower speeds and poor reliability. 5G addresses this by dramatically increasing **capacity**, meaning it can support more devices without reducing performance.

Consider the example of a crowded **music festival**. With 4G, you might struggle to send a text message or upload a photo because the network is overwhelmed by all the people using it at the same time. But with 5G, that congestion is a thing of the past, and everyone at the event can stay connected without issue.

How Does 5G Work?

5G operates on different **frequency bands** than 4G, with several unique components that make its performance so fast and reliable. These components include:

1. **Millimeter Waves (mmWave):**
   - 5G uses **higher frequency bands**, including **millimeter waves**, which are capable of carrying more data over short distances. These waves are used in urban environments and are the reason for those lightning-fast speeds.
   - However, the downside of mmWave is that it doesn't travel as far as lower frequencies, and it's more affected by obstacles like buildings or trees. This means 5G requires a **denser network of cell towers** to make up for the reduced range.
2. **Small Cells:**
   - To overcome the distance limitations of mmWave, 5G relies on **small cells**. These are smaller, more numerous cell towers that help boost coverage, particularly in urban areas.
   - These small cells are placed closer to where you need them—think of them as mini-cell towers, providing ultra-fast internet for smaller areas.
3. **Massive MIMO (Multiple Input, Multiple Output):**
   - MIMO technology uses multiple antennas on a single device or cell tower to send and receive more data simultaneously. **Massive MIMO**, as used in 5G, allows for more antennas and better network performance, making it possible to handle more users and devices at once without compromising speed or reliability.
4. **Beamforming:**

- Beamforming is a technique used to direct signals to specific devices, rather than sending them out in all directions. This results in stronger, more efficient connections that are less prone to interference.
- In a 5G network, beamforming is key to enabling high-speed connections over long distances, especially in urban areas with lots of buildings.

Practical Example: Setting Up 5G at Home

Now, let's see how 5G might be implemented in your own home. Imagine you're looking to upgrade your home internet to a **5G home broadband service**.

Here's how the process would likely work:

1. **Step 1: Check for Availability**
   - First, you need to ensure that 5G service is available in your area. Many mobile carriers are rolling out 5G networks in urban centers first, so if you live in a metropolitan area, there's a good chance that you'll have access to 5G soon, if not already.
2. **Step 2: Choose a 5G Router**
   - If you're upgrading from a 4G network, you'll need a **5G-compatible router**. These routers are designed to connect to 5G networks and provide you with high-speed internet access within your home.
   - For example, companies like **Netgear** and **Samsung** are offering 5G home routers that provide speeds up to **3 Gbps**.
3. **Step 3: Installation**
   - Once you've selected your router, the installation process is straightforward. Most 5G routers come with a quick start guide, allowing you to plug in the device and connect to the 5G network in your area. In some cases, a technician might come to your home to install the equipment and ensure everything is set up properly.
4. **Step 4: Enjoy Faster Internet**
   - After installation, your home will be connected to a 5G network, providing you with fast, reliable internet. Whether

you're streaming ultra-high-definition content, participating in virtual reality experiences, or gaming online, you'll experience **minimal lag** and **faster download speeds**.

Why 5G Matters: The Bigger Picture

While 5G's improvements might seem straightforward, its impact goes beyond just faster internet for consumers. It's about **enabling innovations** in areas like healthcare, autonomous driving, and even entire smart cities. Here's why 5G matters on a broader scale:

- **Healthcare:** Doctors can perform remote surgeries, real-time patient monitoring is possible, and telehealth will reach a new level of efficiency.
- **Autonomous Vehicles:** Cars will communicate with each other and the infrastructure around them, improving road safety and efficiency.
- **Smart Cities:** Traffic systems, power grids, and public services will operate more efficiently and be responsive in real-time.

5G is the foundation for a **hyper-connected future**, where everything from appliances to entire cities can seamlessly communicate with one another. It's the **key enabler** for what's often called the **Internet of Things (IoT)**.

1.2 The Evolution from 1G to 5G

The journey from **1G to 5G** represents the incredible technological evolution of mobile networks and connectivity over the past several decades. Every new generation of mobile technology has brought with it substantial improvements in speed, efficiency, and capacity, each one laying the groundwork for the next. In this section, we'll dive into how each generation has evolved and how the mobile connectivity landscape has transformed over the years, with practical examples to illustrate these changes.

1G - The Beginning of Mobile Communication (1980s)

What is 1G?

1G refers to the first generation of mobile network technology, introduced in the **1980s**. It was revolutionary because, for the first time, it allowed people to make **mobile phone calls** without being tied to a landline. However, **1G was purely analog**, meaning it used analog signals to transmit voice calls, and it wasn't designed to transmit data.

Key Features:

- **Analog technology**: 1G used analog signals for communication, which were susceptible to interference and offered poor call quality.
- **Voice only**: There was no way to send text messages or use mobile data — it was simply voice calls.
- **Limited coverage**: The networks were only available in certain regions and were patchy at best.

Real-World Example:

Imagine calling your friend while driving down the street in the 1980s. You could connect, but the sound quality was often poor, with static or dropped calls. The most advanced technology available at the time allowed people to chat from their cars instead of having to stop at a payphone. That was the extent of 1G's capabilities.

Why 1G Was Limited:

1G had several limitations:

- The analog technology meant that it wasn't secure; anyone with the right equipment could potentially intercept calls.
- The voice quality was unpredictable, especially in areas with lots of interference.
- The mobile devices themselves were bulky and expensive.

2G - The Digital Revolution (1990s)

What is 2G?

2G brought a significant breakthrough in the **1990s**. It switched from analog to **digital technology**, which led to better call quality, the ability to send text messages (SMS), and the beginnings of mobile data services.

Key Features:

- **Digital signals**: Unlike 1G, 2G used digital signals, which allowed for clearer calls and more efficient data transfer.
- **Text messages (SMS)**: 2G enabled the sending of short text messages, allowing users to communicate in new ways.
- **GSM (Global System for Mobile Communications)**: 2G networks were primarily built on GSM technology, which became the standard across most of the world.

Real-World Example:

In the early 1990s, you could send a text message, which was a huge leap forward from the days of 1G. Imagine being able to send a simple "Got your message!" to a friend instead of just calling them. While internet use was still quite limited, the introduction of mobile data was a precursor to the massive growth of smartphones and mobile internet that followed.

Why 2G Was Limited:

While 2G improved the voice and messaging experience, it still had significant limitations:

- **Slow data speeds**: While 2G introduced basic data services (like WAP for browsing the internet), the speeds were extremely slow by today's standards.
- **Limited applications**: It wasn't possible to use mobile devices for much more than basic communication.

3G - The Mobile Internet Revolution (2000s)

What is 3G?

3G marked the beginning of **mobile broadband**. Introduced in the **early 2000s**, it brought substantial improvements in speed, enabling the use of mobile internet on a large scale. It also enabled features like video calls, mobile apps, and faster data transfer, essentially bringing the **internet** to **mobile devices**.

Key Features:

- **Faster data speeds**: 3G provided speeds from **384 Kbps to several Mbps**, which made mobile internet usage practical for the first time.
- **Mobile applications**: With 3G, app stores began to flourish, as users could now download apps that required a stable internet connection.
- **Video calls**: For the first time, 3G allowed for video calling, which paved the way for the popularization of video conferencing apps like Skype.

Real-World Example:

Before 3G, using the internet on your phone was a painful experience. You could barely load a simple website, and if you were lucky, you might be able to send an email. But with 3G, mobile apps like Facebook, YouTube, and Google Maps became practical for everyday use. You could watch videos on YouTube, stream music, and use your phone as a GPS, all thanks to 3G's faster speeds.

Why 3G Was Limited:

While 3G was groundbreaking, it still had limitations:

- **Coverage issues**: 3G networks required more infrastructure, and coverage wasn't always reliable, especially in rural areas.
- **Slower speeds compared to what we expect today**: Video streaming, for instance, wasn't always smooth, and data-hungry applications struggled.

4G - The Smartphone Era (2010s)

What is 4G?

4G took the internet to the next level. With 4G, we saw the beginning of **high-definition video streaming, mobile gaming**, and **real-time social media** on a large scale. 4G provided speeds up to **1 Gbps** under ideal conditions, enabling high-quality media and communication experiences.

Key Features:

- **High-speed data**: 4G allowed for **up to 100 times faster speeds** than 3G, enabling HD video streaming and fast downloads.
- **Low latency**: Reduced latency meant video calls and online gaming could happen with little to no delay.
- **Mobile hotspot capabilities**: 4G also allowed users to share their mobile connection with others, making it easier to get online while on the go.

Real-World Example:

With 4G, services like Netflix, Spotify, and FaceTime became mainstream. Suddenly, you could watch movies on your phone in HD, stream music without interruptions, and have crystal-clear video calls on the go. Think of 4G as the technology that brought **smartphones** to life — it turned them into full-fledged mobile entertainment centers.

Why 4G Was Limited:

While 4G was a leap forward, it still had some drawbacks:

- **Network congestion**: During peak usage times (like at concerts or sports events), 4G networks would slow down because of the massive number of users trying to access data simultaneously.
- **Still not enough for the future**: 4G, while fast, couldn't support the explosive growth of connected devices and data-heavy technologies like **IoT, smart cities**, and **autonomous vehicles**.

5G - The Future of Connectivity (2020s and Beyond)

What is 5G?

Enter **5G** — the **fifth generation** of mobile networks, designed to meet the growing demands of connected societies and industries. 5G is built to be **faster**, **more efficient**, and **more reliable** than any previous network generation. It supports **higher data speeds**, **lower latency**, and **greater device connectivity**, making it the backbone for emerging technologies like **IoT**, **autonomous driving**, and **smart cities**.

Key Features:

- **Gigabit speeds and beyond**: 5G can provide speeds **up to 10 Gbps — 100 times faster than 4G**.
- **Ultra-low latency**: With latency as low as **1 millisecond**, it's nearly instant, enabling real-time applications like remote surgeries, real-time cloud gaming, and autonomous vehicles.
- **Massive device connectivity**: 5G can connect up to **1 million devices per square kilometer**, making it ideal for **IoT**-connected environments like smart cities and factories.

Real-World Example:

Imagine a world where your **self-driving car** communicates with the **traffic lights**, adjusting its speed based on real-time traffic data, avoiding accidents, and finding the fastest route. Meanwhile, in a **smart home**, all your devices — from your thermostat to your fridge to your lighting system — are connected via 5G, communicating and optimizing their performance.

Why 5G Matters:

5G isn't just about speed — it's about enabling a **hyper-connected world**. It's the technology that will make **smart cities** more efficient, **healthcare** more accessible, and **industries** like **manufacturing** and **transportation** more productive and innovative.

The evolution from 1G to 5G is a story of exponential growth, from the basic ability to make voice calls on a mobile phone to a world where virtually everything is connected and optimized in real time. Each generation has built upon the last, progressively enhancing what we can do with mobile networks and setting the stage for future innovations that were once only imagined. As we move forward into the 5G era, the possibilities are boundless.

1.3 Why 5G Matters: A World of Possibilities

As we stand on the brink of the **5G revolution**, it's easy to get excited about the faster speeds and better performance it promises. However, the real question is: **Why does 5G matter?** What makes it such a groundbreaking shift in technology that it's being touted as a game-changer for industries, societies, and our everyday lives?

The Next-Generation Internet: More Than Just Speed

First, let's break down what sets 5G apart from its predecessors. 5G isn't just about downloading movies faster or streaming ultra-HD content without buffering (although those are definitely perks!). It's about enabling a **hyper-connected world** — one where **everything is connected**, from everyday consumer devices to entire cities, industries, and more.

Here's what makes **5G** matter:

1. **Gigabit Speeds and Low Latency:**
   At its core, **5G** is about speed. We're talking speeds that can reach **10 Gbps** (gigabits per second), which is up to **100 times faster than 4G**. This isn't just for downloading files or watching high-definition videos; it's about **enabling real-time communication** between devices that require instantaneous feedback.
2. **Massive Device Connectivity:**
   In a world that's rapidly becoming more connected, 5G will support the connection of up to **1 million devices per square kilometer**. Think about that for a second. In cities, everything — from streetlights to parking meters, from home appliances to wearable health devices — will be able to communicate seamlessly with one another in real-time.

3. **Ultra-low Latency (1 Millisecond):**
   One of the key differentiators of 5G is its **extremely low latency**, which is around **1 millisecond** (compared to 30-50 milliseconds on 4G). This makes 5G the perfect solution for applications that require instant communication, such as **autonomous vehicles**, **remote surgeries**, and **real-time gaming**. With 5G, the lag is almost completely eliminated, making interactions seamless and near-instant.

A New Era for Innovation: How 5G Unlocks New Possibilities

So, how will 5G impact the world beyond the flashy downloads and faster speeds? Let's look at **real-world applications** of 5G across various industries. This is where the **true potential of 5G** starts to shine.

1. Smart Cities: Making Urban Living More Efficient

Imagine a city where traffic lights adjust their timing based on traffic flow, waste bins automatically signal when they're full, and energy grids respond to real-time data to optimize power consumption. This is the promise of **smart cities**, and 5G is the key to making it happen.

With 5G, cities will be able to handle **massive amounts of data** in real-time, allowing them to be more efficient and responsive. From **smart traffic management** that reduces congestion to **remote monitoring** of infrastructure like bridges and roads, 5G will transform urban planning and city management.

Real-Life Example:
In a **smart city**, you could use a mobile app to find an available parking spot in real-time, and as you park, your car could automatically connect to the grid to report its location and update your parking payment. At the same time, the city's energy management system adjusts based on traffic patterns to reduce power consumption.

---

2. Healthcare: A Revolution in Patient Care

The healthcare industry stands to benefit immensely from 5G's capabilities. With its ability to transmit data at lightning speeds and with ultra-low latency, 5G enables a wide range of **telemedicine** innovations, remote surgeries, and real-time health monitoring.

Real-Life Example:
Imagine you live in a rural area far from the nearest hospital. With 5G, a doctor can remotely diagnose your condition, perform a consultation through **real-time video**, and even perform remote surgery using a **robotic surgical system** with precise control. **5G** allows for a **real-time exchange of data** between the doctor and the patient, no matter the physical distance.

Beyond surgery, **wearable devices** that continuously monitor your heart rate, blood pressure, or glucose levels can communicate with medical professionals in real-time. If any abnormal readings are detected, doctors can intervene immediately, ensuring better patient outcomes.

---

3. Autonomous Vehicles: Changing the Future of Transportation

Self-driving cars are no longer a science fiction fantasy. With **5G's low latency** and **high-speed communication**, vehicles can communicate with each other and surrounding infrastructure (such as traffic lights, road sensors, and pedestrians) almost instantaneously.

Real-Life Example:
In a fully connected **autonomous vehicle ecosystem**, your car could receive real-time updates about road conditions, traffic lights, and even potential accidents miles ahead. This allows your car to adjust its speed, make decisions, and avoid obstacles in real-time. A **5G-powered vehicle** could **brake instantly** in response to sudden roadblocks or changes in traffic, reducing accidents and improving safety.

---

4. Manufacturing: The Rise of Smart Factories

Industry 4.0 is the revolution where **smart factories** leverage automation, robotics, and real-time data to optimize production processes. With 5G, the speed and efficiency of machines on the production line will increase exponentially. **5G's low latency** ensures that robots can communicate and adjust their actions in real-time, while **massive device connectivity** allows factory systems to collect and process data more effectively.

Real-Life Example:
In a **smart factory**, robots can assemble products with precision while communicating with sensors that detect any defects in real-time. If a part is damaged or misaligned, the robots adjust their actions automatically to correct the error. Maintenance workers can also be alerted to potential machine malfunctions **before they occur**, preventing costly downtime.

---

5. Entertainment and Gaming: Real-Time Immersion

For the entertainment and gaming industries, **5G** is the ticket to a **new level of interactivity**. With 5G, high-definition video streaming, **augmented reality (AR)**, and **virtual reality (VR)** experiences will become more immersive and responsive than ever.

Real-Life Example:
Imagine playing a **cloud-based game** with friends, where your game character seamlessly interacts with others in **real-time**. Unlike 4G, which might cause lag or interruptions, 5G ensures smooth and responsive gameplay. In the world of **virtual reality**, 5G enables incredibly realistic simulations where users can interact in real-time with virtual worlds without experiencing motion sickness or delays.

5G for Business: Enabling New Business Models and Opportunities

5G doesn't just improve existing services — it will **open new business opportunities** that were previously not possible due to the constraints of older network technologies.

For example:

- **Retailers** can use **AR** to provide customers with virtual shopping experiences, where they can try on clothes virtually or view how furniture will look in their homes.
- **Supply chains** can be streamlined with **real-time data**, allowing for predictive maintenance, just-in-time inventory, and optimized deliveries.
- **Remote work** will become even more efficient, with high-quality video conferences, instant file sharing, and real-time collaboration tools that feel just like being in the same room.

The Bottom Line: Why 5G Matters

While it's tempting to focus on the speed and performance aspects of 5G, its true value lies in its ability to **unlock new possibilities** that will redefine how we live and work. From transforming industries to enabling entirely new business models, 5G is set to be the foundation of **innovations** we haven't even imagined yet.

The impact of 5G will be felt not just in consumer applications, but across healthcare, transportation, manufacturing, entertainment, and beyond. It's the **next frontier of digital connectivity**, and the possibilities are virtually limitless.

In short, **5G matters** because it will **reshape the future**. From transforming cities into smarter, more efficient places to enabling a world of instant communication, automation, and innovation, 5G will fundamentally change our everyday lives and our businesses for the better.

Chapter 2: The Core Technology Behind 5G

Understanding **5G** isn't just about knowing the benefits, like faster speeds and lower latency. To truly appreciate its power and potential, it's important to dive into the technology that makes 5G tick. In this chapter, we'll explore the **core technologies** that enable 5G, including **radio waves**, **small cells**, **MIMO (Multiple Input, Multiple Output)**, and **millimeter waves**. By the end of this chapter, you'll have a clear understanding of how these technologies work together to create the next-generation mobile network.

2.1 Radio Waves and Frequency Bands

To understand how **5G** works, it's essential to understand the building blocks of wireless communication: **radio waves** and **frequency bands**. These elements are the foundation upon which all wireless networks are built, including the mobile networks we use every day. In this section, we'll break down these concepts in detail, explaining how they work, why they matter for 5G, and how they enable faster, more efficient connectivity.

What Are Radio Waves?

Let's start with the basics. **Radio waves** are a type of **electromagnetic wave**, just like visible light, microwaves, or X-rays. All these waves travel through the air (or vacuum) at the speed of light, but they differ in terms of their **wavelengths** and **frequencies**.

- **Wavelength** is the distance between one peak of a wave and the next peak.
- **Frequency** refers to how many times a wave passes a given point per second.

In simpler terms, **radio waves** are just a form of **electromagnetic radiation** that carry information (such as phone calls, text messages, and internet data) through the air. **5G** uses radio waves to transmit data to and from devices, like smartphones, routers, and base stations (cell towers).

Why Do Radio Waves Matter for 5G?

For **5G networks**, **radio waves** play a critical role because they're used to carry the massive amounts of data required to support things like **video streaming**, **gaming**, and **smart cities**. To enable faster speeds and more reliable connections, **5G** uses **higher frequency radio waves** than previous generations of mobile networks.

But here's the twist: while **higher-frequency radio waves** can carry more data, they also have a **shorter range** and are more easily blocked by obstacles like buildings, trees, and even rain. That's why **5G** requires a denser infrastructure of cell towers and small cells compared to earlier networks.

Frequency Bands: The Roadways of Wireless Communication

Now, let's talk about **frequency bands**. The radio spectrum is divided into different frequency bands that are allocated for various uses, including broadcasting, satellite communication, Wi-Fi, and mobile networks. These frequency bands are **chunks** of the electromagnetic spectrum, and the government (or relevant regulatory bodies) assigns these bands to different types of communication services.

Radio Spectrum Allocation

Imagine the radio spectrum as a **highway** system, where different **lanes** (frequency bands) are reserved for specific types of communication. For example:

- **AM/FM radio** uses certain bands of the spectrum.
- **Wi-Fi** uses different bands (typically 2.4 GHz and 5 GHz).
- **Mobile networks** use specific bands for 2G, 3G, 4G, and 5G.

Each **frequency band** has its **own characteristics** that make it suited for different uses:

- **Low-frequency bands** (below 1 GHz) can travel long distances and pass through obstacles like buildings, but they carry less data.
- **Mid-frequency bands** (1 GHz to 6 GHz) offer a balance between speed and coverage.
- **High-frequency bands** (above 6 GHz, including millimeter waves) can carry huge amounts of data but have limited range and are more easily blocked by obstacles.

How Frequency Bands Impact 5G

For **5G**, we are using a **wide range of frequency bands**, which allow the network to deliver the speeds, capacity, and low latency that are expected of next-generation technology. 5G is designed to use both **sub-6 GHz frequencies** for broad coverage and **millimeter waves (24 GHz and above)** for ultra-fast data transfer.

Real-World Example: Think of **low-frequency bands** as the lanes on a highway that can fit large numbers of cars traveling long distances but at slower speeds. These are great for rural areas where wide coverage is needed, like **4G LTE** networks. On the other hand, **millimeter waves** are more like **express lanes** where cars can zoom past at much higher speeds, but the lanes are narrower and not as many cars can fit in at once. Millimeter waves enable **extremely high-speed data transfer**, but they are used primarily in **high-density areas** like city centers or stadiums, where lots of devices need to connect at once.

Sub-6 GHz Bands: The Backbone of 5G Coverage

The **sub-6 GHz** frequency range is one of the most important bands for **5G networks**. These frequencies are crucial because they provide a balance between **coverage** and **speed**. They allow **5G** networks to offer wide coverage while still delivering fast speeds, making them ideal for both **urban and rural areas**.

Sub-6 GHz for Global 5G Rollout

One of the key reasons why **sub-6 GHz** bands are so important is that they offer a more **globally compatible solution** for 5G. Many countries are rolling out 5G using these frequencies because they're capable of providing **broad coverage** while ensuring compatibility across regions. For example:

- **China**, **South Korea**, and many parts of **Europe** are rolling out 5G using **sub-6 GHz bands** for wide-area coverage.
- These frequencies are especially useful in **rural areas** where a long-range signal is needed, and the data demands are lower compared to city centers.

Millimeter Waves: The Ultra-Fast Highway of 5G

One of the most exciting aspects of **5G** is the use of **millimeter waves (mmWaves)**, which are frequencies in the range of **24 GHz and above**. Millimeter waves are a **key enabler** for **5G**, as they provide **extremely fast data speeds**, which are ideal for applications like **4K/8K video streaming**, **real-time gaming**, and **augmented reality (AR)**.

Why Millimeter Waves Matter

Millimeter waves have a **shorter wavelength**, which allows them to carry more data and offer higher frequencies. However, their **range** is limited, and they can be blocked easily by physical obstacles (buildings, trees, even weather conditions like rain).

In practical terms:

- **5G networks** use **small cells** (miniature cell towers) and **beamforming** technology to **boost the signal** and direct it toward devices that need the connection. This helps overcome the limitations of **mmWave frequencies** in urban areas.
- **Real-world example**: In a **stadium** with thousands of people watching a live concert, mmWaves can provide ultra-fast speeds for users to stream high-definition video without buffering, while **small cells** placed around the stadium ensure that the signal reaches everyone.

Challenges with Millimeter Waves

While **mmWaves** offer incredible speeds, they are more vulnerable to interference and signal degradation due to their **shorter range**. They require a dense infrastructure of **small cells** to ensure coverage, which is why **5G networks** in cities will rely on many small, localized cell stations, rather than the large towers that 4G uses.

Practical Examples of Frequency Bands in 5G Networks

1. **Urban Areas**: In a **city center**, 5G networks will often rely on **millimeter waves** to deliver ultra-fast data speeds. These high-frequency bands can transmit data quickly but will require **small cells** and **beamforming** to overcome obstacles like tall buildings.
2. **Rural Areas**: In less densely populated areas, **sub-6 GHz** frequencies are better suited for **broad coverage**. These frequencies offer **longer-range signals** and are less prone to interference, making them ideal for areas with fewer users and more open space.
3. **Dense Venues**: In a **sports stadium** or a **concert hall**, where thousands of people may be streaming video at the same time, **5G** can use **millimeter waves** to handle the **high data demand**. **Small cells** will be placed throughout the venue to ensure high-speed connectivity across the crowd.

The success of **5G** depends largely on the use of **radio waves** and **frequency bands**. By utilizing a wide range of frequencies — from **sub-6 GHz** for coverage to **millimeter waves** for speed — **5G networks** can offer both **broad coverage** and **high-speed data transfer**, making them suitable for **urban** and **rural areas** alike.

The combination of **advanced technologies** like **small cells, MIMO**, and **beamforming** allows 5G to maximize the potential of these frequency bands, overcoming the limitations of **higher-frequency signals** while delivering **fast, reliable** internet to users in even the most densely populated locations.

2.2 Small Cells and MIMO Technology

When it comes to enabling the lightning-fast speeds, massive capacity, and ultra-low latency that 5G promises, two key technologies play a central role: **small cells** and **MIMO technology**. These two elements are the building blocks that allow 5G networks to perform at their highest potential, especially in crowded environments like urban centers, stadiums, and other high-demand areas.

Small Cells: Boosting Coverage and Capacity

What Are Small Cells?

In the context of 5G, **small cells** are low-power, short-range base stations that provide wireless coverage in specific areas. Unlike traditional **macro cells** (the large towers you often see dotting the landscape), which provide coverage over large distances, small cells are designed to provide high-speed data in more localized areas.

Think of small cells as **miniature cell towers** that are scattered throughout a city or dense environment. They typically cover a smaller area but play a crucial role in ensuring that there's no dead zone in high-traffic locations, like stadiums, shopping malls, or urban streets.

Why Do Small Cells Matter?

One of the major challenges 5G faces is the **short range** of higher-frequency radio waves, such as those used in **millimeter waves**. These waves are capable of delivering **blazing-fast speeds**, but they don't travel very far and are easily blocked by obstacles like buildings, trees, or even rain. This is where small cells come into play.

By deploying small cells in strategic locations, **5G networks** can provide **reliable, high-speed coverage** even in places where larger towers might struggle to reach.

Real-World Example:
Imagine you're at a crowded concert in a large arena. Everyone is trying to use their phones to stream live videos, check social media, and share photos. The demand for data is sky-high, and the existing cellular network might not be able to handle the load, leading to slow speeds and dropped connections.

By deploying **small cells** throughout the venue, the network can handle the massive data demands of thousands of concertgoers at the same time. These small cells provide localized coverage and connect directly to the core network, ensuring that each device has a strong, reliable connection.

Where Are Small Cells Used?

Small cells are used in environments where high demand and **high-density coverage** are needed. Examples include:

- **Stadiums and Arenas**: Ensuring that thousands of fans can access the network without congestion.
- **Urban Areas**: Placing small cells along busy streets to improve connectivity in city centers.
- **Shopping Malls and Airports**: Offering high-speed data in places where large numbers of people gather.
- **Residential Areas**: Improving coverage and speed for home users in rural or suburban areas.

MIMO Technology: Maximizing Data Throughput

What is MIMO (Multiple Input, Multiple Output)?

MIMO stands for **Multiple Input, Multiple Output**. It's a technology used in wireless communication systems to increase data throughput and system capacity by using multiple antennas at both the transmitter and receiver.

In traditional systems, a single antenna on the cell tower would send a signal, and the mobile device would receive it with a single antenna. However, MIMO uses multiple antennas to send and receive data simultaneously. By doing so, it can transmit multiple data streams at once, vastly improving the overall performance of the network.

How Does MIMO Work in 5G?

In **5G, MIMO technology** is taken to the next level with a feature known as **massive MIMO**. Instead of just a handful of antennas, **massive MIMO** involves using **hundreds or even thousands of antennas** to simultaneously send and receive data. This dramatically increases the **capacity** and **efficiency** of the network.

Here's how it works:

- **Multiple Antennas**: A typical MIMO system uses multiple antennas at both the base station and the device (such as your smartphone or router) to send and receive data in parallel.
- **Beamforming**: MIMO technology works in tandem with **beamforming** (another core 5G technology), which allows the antennas to focus their signal in the direction of the user. This improves **signal strength** and reduces interference from other sources.
- **Spatial Multiplexing**: This is the technique where multiple data streams are transmitted simultaneously on the same frequency, effectively increasing the data throughput.

Why MIMO is Crucial for 5G

Without MIMO, 5G wouldn't be able to achieve the high data rates that we expect. By using **multiple antennas** and **beamforming**, 5G can maximize the efficiency of each frequency band and ensure that more users can be supported simultaneously without compromising performance.

Real-World Example: Let's say you're in a busy subway station with hundreds of people all trying to use their phones at the same time. Without MIMO, the system would have to handle each device one at a time, leading to congestion and slower speeds.

With **MIMO**, the network can handle multiple data streams simultaneously, sending data to several users at once. If there are **hundreds of users**, the network uses its multiple antennas to efficiently distribute the load and maintain high speeds for everyone, ensuring a **smooth and uninterrupted experience**.

Massive MIMO in 5G

With **massive MIMO**, the technology is scaled up. **5G** uses **large antenna arrays** (up to hundreds of antennas on a single base station), which allows for **advanced beamforming** and the simultaneous transmission of many more data streams. This results in **greater capacity**, improved **network efficiency**, and the ability to deliver high-speed data even in **dense environments** with lots of devices connected at once.

Real-World Example: Consider a **high-traffic airport** where passengers are using their phones, laptops, and other devices. The use of **massive MIMO** allows the network to efficiently allocate bandwidth to all users, delivering **high-speed connections** without any slowdowns, even when the network is under heavy load.

How Small Cells and MIMO Work Together

Both **small cells** and **MIMO technology** play complementary roles in delivering a high-performing 5G network. Here's how they work together:

- **Small cells** help deliver high-speed, low-latency coverage to localized areas, making sure that the signal doesn't drop when you're on the go. They're especially useful in **dense environments** like stadiums, concert venues, or city centers.
- **MIMO technology**, particularly **massive MIMO**, increases the data throughput and capacity of the network, ensuring that the small cells can handle the massive data demands of multiple users simultaneously.

In practical terms, **small cells** provide the localized, high-speed connectivity, while **MIMO** maximizes the data flow and efficiency, ensuring that the network can handle multiple devices without compromising performance.

Both **small cells** and **MIMO technology** are vital for enabling the **high-speed, high-capacity, and low-latency** experiences that we expect from 5G. Small cells ensure that 5G's coverage is pervasive and reliable, even in the densest environments, while MIMO maximizes the efficiency of the network by increasing its capacity and data throughput.

Together, they form the backbone of 5G's ability to serve the **massive demand** for data in urban areas, high-traffic venues, and industrial environments. As 5G continues to roll out, these technologies will be deployed in more places, ensuring that users across the globe can experience the true potential of next-generation connectivity.

2.3 Millimeter Waves and Their Role in 5G

When you think of **5G**, one of the most exciting components that comes to mind is likely **speed**. The blazing-fast data transfer speeds that 5G promises are made possible, in large part, by the use of **millimeter waves (mmWaves)**. These waves are one of the defining features of **5G technology**, enabling it to support high-bandwidth applications like **4K video streaming**, **augmented reality (AR)**, and **virtual reality (VR)**.

But what exactly are millimeter waves, and why are they so important for 5G? In this section, we'll break down **mmWaves**, explain how they work, and discuss their role in 5G networks. We'll also cover some practical examples and real-world implementations to help you understand how this technology is already transforming our world.

What Are Millimeter Waves?

Millimeter waves are a subset of the **radio frequency spectrum** that operate at **frequencies between 24 GHz and 100 GHz**. The name **"millimeter"** comes from the fact that the wavelength of these waves is measured in millimeters (hence the term "millimeter wave"). To put it into perspective, these wavelengths are much smaller than the wavelengths used in lower frequency bands like **sub-6 GHz**, which have longer wavelengths.

Characteristics of Millimeter Waves:

- **Higher Frequencies**: Millimeter waves operate at much higher frequencies compared to the traditional frequencies used in previous generations (like 4G). This allows them to carry significantly more data.
- **Shorter Range**: While mmWaves are capable of transmitting vast amounts of data, they have a **shorter range** than lower-frequency waves. This makes them ideal for urban environments where users need ultra-fast data speeds over short distances.
- **Susceptible to Interference**: Millimeter waves are more easily blocked by obstacles like buildings, trees, and even weather conditions like rain. This is a key consideration in deploying **5G** networks that rely on mmWaves for high-speed data transmission.

How Millimeter Waves Enable 5G

The key advantage of **mmWaves** is their ability to provide **high-speed data transfer** and **large bandwidth**. In the context of **5G**, mmWaves are essential for **delivering the ultra-fast speeds** that 5G promises, especially in **high-density urban areas** where many devices are connected simultaneously.

Why Are Millimeter Waves Essential for 5G?

To understand why **mmWaves** are critical for **5G**, let's compare them to the lower-frequency waves that 4G networks use:

1. **Speed**: Lower-frequency waves (like those used in 4G) are capable of supporting basic mobile communication, but they have limited bandwidth. **Millimeter waves**, on the other hand, have **much more bandwidth**, which allows them to support **data-heavy applications** like **HD video streaming**, **cloud gaming**, and **IoT** (Internet of Things) networks.
2. **Latency**: With their ability to transmit data over short distances quickly, **mmWaves** reduce **latency** — the delay between sending

and receiving data. For applications requiring **real-time interaction**, like **autonomous vehicles** or **remote surgery**, this low-latency feature of **5G** is essential.

3. **Capacity**: **5G networks** use **mmWaves** to handle **large amounts of data** simultaneously. This makes them perfect for areas with **high device density** like stadiums, shopping malls, or urban centers where thousands of people are trying to connect to the network at the same time.

Challenges of Millimeter Waves:

While **millimeter waves** offer **incredible speed and capacity**, they also have some challenges, particularly in terms of their **range** and **penetration abilities**. Let's go over these challenges and how **5G** addresses them.

1. Shorter Range and Line-of-Sight Requirements

Millimeter waves can travel only short distances, and their signal strength drops significantly when they encounter physical barriers like buildings, trees, or even rain. This makes them less suitable for **long-distance communication**, and also means they have trouble penetrating through materials like walls.

- **How 5G Solves This**: To overcome this, **5G networks** use a **dense network of small cells** that are placed closer to users and more frequently than traditional cell towers. These small cells act as **mini cell towers** that help deliver **strong and consistent signals** in high-demand areas.

2. Interference from Weather

Millimeter waves can be absorbed or scattered by **rain, fog**, and even **humidity**. This limits their effectiveness in certain weather conditions.

- **How 5G Solves This**: To mitigate weather interference, **5G systems** deploy **multiple small cells** to ensure a **robust signal** even if some mmWave signals are blocked or degraded. The use of **lower-frequency bands** (sub-6 GHz) alongside **millimeter waves** also ensures that coverage is available even in more challenging weather.

3. High Power Consumption

Because mmWaves require **large antenna arrays** (such as those in **massive MIMO systems**) and small cells, they often demand more power to function efficiently.

- **How 5G Solves This**: As **5G networks** evolve, new **power-efficient designs** for small cells and antennas are being developed to ensure that the network remains energy-efficient while maintaining its performance.

Practical Example: How Millimeter Waves Work in Real-World 5G Deployments

Let's explore how **millimeter waves** are already being used in **real-world 5G networks**.

Urban City Centers:

In dense urban areas, **5G networks** are using **millimeter waves** to deliver ultra-fast internet speeds to **smartphones, laptops**, and **connected devices**. These networks rely on a combination of **small cells** and **massive MIMO antennas** to ensure that the signal doesn't drop, even in high-density areas where there are many obstacles like buildings.

- **Example**: In **New York City, Verizon** deployed **mmWave-based 5G** in select neighborhoods, using **small cells** to boost coverage in high-traffic areas like Times Square. The **mmWave** signals provide fast downloads and a consistent experience for people in busy areas where large amounts of data are being used simultaneously.

Stadiums and Concert Venues:

When tens of thousands of people gather in one place, like in **sports stadiums** or **concert venues**, the demand for mobile data skyrockets. To ensure smooth, high-speed connectivity for all users, these venues use **mmWave technology** to handle the massive influx of data.

- **Example**: The **Mercedes-Benz Stadium** in Atlanta, home to the **Atlanta Falcons**, is an excellent example of a **5G-enabled stadium**. By using **mmWave frequencies**, the stadium can provide ultra-fast speeds to thousands of fans simultaneously. Whether it's for streaming the game in high-definition or uploading content to social media, **mmWaves** ensure the network can handle the load.

Autonomous Vehicles:

In the world of **autonomous vehicles**, where quick decisions are critical to safety, **low-latency communication** is a must. **Millimeter waves** play a key role in enabling **5G** to deliver real-time information exchange between **vehicles**, **traffic signals**, and **infrastructure**.

- **Example**: In **smart city environments, mmWave-based 5G** networks allow **autonomous cars** to communicate with each other and with traffic systems to make real-time decisions based on **live data**. For example, a self-driving car can instantly receive updates on road conditions, pedestrian movements, and even traffic light changes, all made possible by **5G and millimeter waves**.

Millimeter waves are one of the most exciting and crucial components of **5G technology**. By enabling **ultra-fast data transmission** and **low-latency communications**, they allow for the seamless and high-speed experiences that **5G** is known for. However, mmWaves come with challenges, including shorter range and susceptibility to interference, which 5G solves through **dense small cell deployments** and **advanced beamforming techniques**.

As 5G continues to evolve, **millimeter waves** will be a central part of the network's ability to handle the growing demands for **high-speed data**, **massive device connectivity**, and **real-time communication**. They will be integral to making technologies like **autonomous vehicles, smart cities, remote surgeries**, and **immersive entertainment** a reality.

Chapter 3: Key Differences Between 4G and 5G

The world of mobile networks has come a long way since the introduction of 4G, and now we're standing at the threshold of a **new era** — **5G**. But what exactly sets **5G** apart from **4G**? In this chapter, we'll dive into the **key differences between 4G and 5G** across several crucial areas: **speed**, **latency**, **device density**, and **network efficiency**. We'll also look at how these improvements will directly impact **consumers**, giving you a practical understanding of what to expect as 5G becomes more widespread.

3.1 Speed and Latency: A Quantum Leap

When it comes to **5G**, the most frequently mentioned improvements over **4G** are its **speed** and **latency**. These two factors are key to understanding why **5G** is such a game-changer and why it promises to unlock a range of exciting new possibilities across industries and for consumers.

Understanding Speed: The Need for Blazing Fast Connectivity

At its core, **speed** refers to how quickly data can travel from one point to another. It is often measured in **megabits per second (Mbps)** or **gigabits per second (Gbps)**. Higher numbers mean faster internet, which leads to smoother streaming, quicker downloads, and faster uploads.

4G vs. 5G Speeds

- **4G Speeds**: **4G LTE**, the network most people use today, offers speeds between **10 Mbps to 100 Mbps**, depending on your location, signal strength, and network congestion. With these speeds, you can stream **HD video**, download apps, and browse the web with relatively good performance. However, for **data-heavy** applications like **4K streaming** or **cloud gaming**, 4G can sometimes fall short, especially in crowded areas.

- **5G Speeds**: **5G**, on the other hand, promises speeds of up to **10 Gbps** in ideal conditions, which is up to **100 times faster** than 4G. To put that into perspective, **5G** could download a **full-length HD movie** in about **3 seconds**, while **4G** might take around **5 minutes** for the same file. Imagine trying to download **large files**, stream **high-definition content**, or participate in **real-time applications** with **virtually no waiting** — that's the reality **5G** enables.

Real-World Example:

Let's say you're a content creator and you regularly upload large video files to YouTube. With **4G**, you might experience delays during the upload process, especially when working with **4K videos**. On **5G**, you'll be able to upload that same **4K video** in a fraction of the time, making the process much faster and more efficient.

For consumers, this means **lightning-fast downloads**, **buffer-free streaming**, and a **smooth user experience** even in **high-demand situations**.

Understanding Latency: Reducing the Delay in Communication

Latency is the amount of time it takes for data to travel from one point to another, often referred to as the **"delay"**. It's measured in milliseconds (ms), and lower latency means faster response times. **Latency** is especially important for applications that require **instant feedback**, such as **online gaming**, **video calls**, and **autonomous vehicles**.

4G vs. 5G Latency

- **4G Latency**: **4G** has a latency of around **30-50 milliseconds**. While this is good enough for most tasks, it can cause noticeable lag when performing real-time activities. For example, if you're playing a **fast-paced multiplayer game**, you may experience delays between pressing buttons and seeing the result on your screen. Similarly, in **video calls**, there might be a slight delay between when someone speaks and when you hear them.

- **5G Latency**: **5G** dramatically reduces this latency to as low as **1 millisecond**. This is a **quantum leap** in performance, making real-time communication near-instantaneous. Imagine being able to send and receive data with virtually **no delay** — this is **5G's** big advantage.

Real-World Example:

Consider **remote surgery**. In **4G**, the delay between the surgeon's movements and the robot's responses might be too long to ensure precision, especially in a high-stakes environment like surgery. With **5G**, the surgeon can perform actions in **real-time**, with a **delay of just milliseconds**. This opens up new possibilities for performing surgeries remotely, especially in **rural or underserved areas** where access to specialists may be limited.

Similarly, in **autonomous vehicles**, **5G's low latency** will allow **vehicles** to communicate with each other and their environment (traffic lights, pedestrians, road signs) almost **instantaneously**, making the **roads safer** and allowing **self-driving cars** to make better decisions in real time.

Why Speed and Latency Matter for 5G's Future

Now that we've looked at **what speed** and **latency** are, let's explore why they are **crucial for 5G** and the **future of connectivity**.

The Growing Demand for Data

As technology evolves, so do our **data needs**. The rise of **4K/8K video, virtual reality (VR), augmented reality (AR), cloud gaming**, and other **data-heavy applications** demands much more bandwidth than previous generations of networks could provide. **5G** was designed to meet this demand.

- **High-Speed Applications**: With **5G**, users will be able to enjoy applications like **4K streaming** or **cloud gaming** without interruptions. For instance, imagine watching a live sports event in

4K or playing an intense **multiplayer game** in real-time, with no buffering or lag.

Real-Time Experiences

For **real-time experiences** like **autonomous driving**, **remote surgeries**, or **smart cities**, **low latency** is absolutely critical. Whether it's enabling vehicles to avoid collisions or making sure that a surgeon can control a robotic arm without delay, **5G's low latency** is the key to making these experiences **safe and reliable**.

Increased Device Connectivity

As we continue to see the proliferation of **IoT devices** (smart homes, wearables, connected cars, etc.), **5G's high speed and low latency** will ensure that all these devices can function effectively at the same time. **5G** will allow **millions of devices** to communicate with each other without overwhelming the network, ensuring that everything from your **smart thermostat** to your **fitness tracker** operates efficiently.

Practical Implementations and Real-World Impact

So, what does this all mean for consumers and businesses? Here are some examples of how **5G's speed and low latency** will impact the real world:

1. Streaming and Entertainment

- **5G** will enable **seamless streaming** of **4K and 8K content** without buffering, offering users a much higher-quality viewing experience.
- Consumers will be able to watch **live sports** or concerts in **virtual reality** with real-time interaction, making entertainment more immersive than ever.

2. Autonomous Vehicles

- **Self-driving cars** will be able to exchange information with other vehicles and infrastructure in **real-time**, making roads safer and reducing traffic accidents. For example, **5G's low latency** allows vehicles to react immediately to road hazards, making driving safer and more efficient.

3. Smart Cities

- **Smart traffic management** will be enabled by **5G's speed and low latency**. Traffic lights will adjust in real-time based on traffic flow, reducing congestion and improving overall city efficiency. **Waste management systems** will detect when bins are full and automatically schedule pickups, optimizing resources.

4. Healthcare

- In the medical field, **5G's low latency** will enable **remote surgeries** where surgeons can control robotic arms in real-time, as well as the **real-time monitoring** of patients' health data, leading to better and faster diagnosis and treatment.

5. Virtual and Augmented Reality

- **VR and AR** will become much more responsive, providing smooth, immersive experiences that are key for gaming, remote work, and educational applications. For example, **5G** will make it possible to participate in **virtual conferences** or **AR-guided repair services** without lag or interruptions.

3.2 Device Density and Network Efficiency

One of the most exciting features of **5G** technology is its ability to handle **massive device density**. As we become more connected, with the rise of the **Internet of Things (IoT)**, the number of connected devices is exploding. From smart homes to **wearables, self-driving cars**, and **smart cities**, the demand for connectivity is higher than ever before. But how do networks manage this overwhelming increase in the number of connected devices? That's where **device density** and **network efficiency** come into play.

What is Device Density?

Device density refers to the number of devices that a network can handle within a specific area, measured per square kilometer. With the rise of connected devices in our daily lives, especially in **urban environments** or **event venues**, networks must be able to support an ever-growing number of devices without **compromising performance**.

4G's Device Density Limitations

With **4G networks**, the number of devices per square kilometer that could be supported was limited to about **100,000 devices**. While this worked well for individual smartphone users, the **increasing number of connected devices**—from **smartphones** to **IoT devices** like **smart thermostats**, **fitness trackers**, and **connected cars**—was beginning to push the limits of traditional networks.

- **Real-World Example**: At a **concert** or a **sports stadium**, where **thousands of people** are trying to stream live video, upload pictures, or send messages at the same time, the network can get congested. This results in slower speeds, dropped connections, and frustration for users.

5G's Ability to Handle High Device Density

5G, on the other hand, was designed from the ground up to **support up to 1 million devices per square kilometer**. That's a significant leap — **10 times more devices** than what **4G** can handle. This is especially important as we move toward **smarter cities**, **connected homes**, and **autonomous vehicles**, all of which rely on a dense network of interconnected devices.

With **5G's high capacity**, **more devices** can be connected simultaneously without reducing the **overall network speed** or **efficiency**. This is crucial for environments where there are **high concentrations of users** and connected devices, such as in **stadiums**, **concerts**, **airports**, and **city centers**.

Why Network Efficiency Matters for 5G

To manage this **massive increase in device density**, **5G networks** need to be highly efficient. This involves the **optimal use of network resources**, such as **frequency bands, network traffic management**, and **dynamic allocation of bandwidth**, to ensure that the network can handle a large volume of devices while delivering high performance.

4G vs. 5G Network Efficiency

- **4G**: **4G networks** were designed to support traditional mobile services like voice calls and web browsing. While it can handle some **data-heavy applications**, it struggles when there's **high traffic** or a large number of devices. For example, during a **sports event**, **4G networks** can become congested, resulting in **slower speeds** for users.
- **5G**: 5G, with its **improved efficiency**, can handle **more devices simultaneously** and **optimize bandwidth allocation** dynamically based on demand. Whether you're in a densely populated city, at a concert, or driving through a busy highway, **5G networks** will adjust their resources efficiently to ensure each device gets the best possible experience.

How 5G Achieves High Device Density and Network Efficiency

Let's now break down the **key technologies** that **5G** uses to achieve **high device density** and **network efficiency**.

1. Small Cells

As we discussed earlier, **small cells** are miniature base stations that provide **localized coverage**. These cells can be deployed densely throughout an area, such as along a busy street or inside a stadium, ensuring that the network can handle many more devices in a given area.

By distributing **small cells** more frequently than traditional **macro towers**, 5G can efficiently manage device connections and ensure that even in crowded locations, the signal is strong and reliable.

Real-World Example:
Imagine you're in a busy **airport terminal**, with hundreds of passengers using their phones at the same time. Without **small cells**, the network would struggle to handle the massive volume of users. But with **small cells** deployed throughout the airport, **5G** can keep each passenger's device connected without slowing down the network.

2. Massive MIMO

We touched on **MIMO (Multiple Input, Multiple Output)** technology in an earlier chapter, but let's look at it again in the context of device density. **MIMO** technology uses **multiple antennas** at both the base station and on your device to increase the number of data streams that can be sent and received simultaneously. This increases the **overall capacity** of the network.

In **5G**, **massive MIMO** is used, which involves using **hundreds or even thousands of antennas** at the base station to maximize the **data throughput**. This allows **5G** to support **more devices at once**, without sacrificing performance.

Real-World Example:
At a **sports stadium**, where tens of thousands of fans are simultaneously using their devices to upload photos, stream videos, or access information, **massive MIMO** ensures that the network can handle all these devices without experiencing congestion or slowdown. Each antenna helps distribute the data load evenly, ensuring a **smooth experience** for everyone.

3. Network Slicing

Network slicing is a key technology that allows **5G** to optimize **network efficiency** by **creating virtual networks** within the physical 5G infrastructure. These virtual networks, or **slices**, can be tailored to meet the specific needs of different applications, users, or devices.

For example:

- One slice of the network can be dedicated to **autonomous vehicles**, ensuring **low latency** and **high reliability**.
- Another slice could be optimized for **smart homes**, prioritizing devices like security cameras, thermostats, and smart lights.
- A third slice might be reserved for **high-bandwidth applications**, such as **4K streaming** or **cloud gaming**.

By efficiently allocating resources through **network slicing**, **5G networks** can prioritize traffic, minimize congestion, and ensure that all devices get the performance they need.

Real-World Example:
In a **smart city**, **network slicing** can ensure that **emergency services** get priority bandwidth, while **consumer devices** like smartphones and IoT devices receive optimized connectivity based on demand. If there's an **emergency situation**, the network can quickly allocate more resources to support things like **ambulances**, **drones**, and **public safety systems**.

4. Beamforming

Beamforming is a technique that allows antennas to focus their signal on specific devices or areas, rather than broadcasting in all directions. This helps to **optimize coverage**, increase **signal strength**, and reduce interference.

In **5G**, **beamforming** is used alongside **massive MIMO** to **direct** the signal where it's needed most. This allows the network to be more **efficient** by reducing the amount of interference and ensuring that devices are receiving strong, reliable signals.

Real-World Example:
During a **concert**, many people are connected to the **5G network**, all of them using their phones to post social media updates, stream live videos, or check event details. With **beamforming**, the network can focus the signal directly on the crowd or specific users, ensuring that everyone stays connected without overwhelming the network.

Real-World Impact: What Consumers Can Expect

The key improvements in **device density** and **network efficiency** mean that **5G** will provide a much smoother, more reliable experience for consumers, even in crowded environments. Here's what consumers can expect:

1. **Better Coverage in Crowded Areas**: Whether you're at a **sports game**, a **music festival**, or even just in a busy **city center**, **5G** will ensure that you have **fast, reliable connectivity**. No more slow speeds or dropped calls during peak times.
2. **Improved IoT Connectivity**: With **millions of devices** connected to the **5G network** in smart cities, homes, and industries, you'll experience seamless interactions between **connected devices**. From **smart thermostats** to **autonomous vehicles**, **5G** will make sure everything works together without missing a beat.
3. **No More Network Congestion**: With **5G**, even if everyone around you is using their phone to stream video or browse social media, you won't have to deal with **slower speeds** or **poor connections**. Thanks to **small cells**, **massive MIMO**, and **beamforming**, **5G networks** will be able to handle large amounts of data without slowing down.

3.3 Real-World Impact: What Consumers Can Expect

As **5G** technology becomes more widespread, the question on many people's minds is: **What does 5G mean for me as a consumer?** In this section, we'll break down how **5G's improvements in speed, latency, device density, and network efficiency** will translate into tangible benefits for everyday users. Whether you're at home, at work, or on the go, **5G** will bring changes to the way you experience technology.

We'll also look at **real-world applications** where **5G** will make a noticeable difference and highlight how different sectors of society will benefit. Finally, we'll address some **practical examples** to show how **5G** will become a vital part of everyday life.

1. Faster, Seamless Internet Experiences

One of the most immediate changes that **5G** brings to consumers is the **dramatic increase in speed**. If you've ever experienced the frustration of slow download speeds, video buffering, or lag during gaming, **5G** will make those issues a thing of the past.

How 5G Makes a Difference:

- **Faster Downloads**: Downloading a large movie or high-quality video on **4G** might take several minutes, but with **5G**, the same content can be downloaded in just a few seconds. Think about **downloading 10 GB files** in under 10 seconds.
- **Buffer-Free Streaming**: Whether you're streaming **4K video**, watching a **live event**, or enjoying your favorite **streaming platform**, **5G** ensures that the video will load instantly without any buffering or delays.
- **Faster Uploads**: For content creators who upload videos, photos, or large files, **5G** will provide upload speeds that are much faster than **4G**, reducing the time spent waiting for large files to go live.

Real-World Example: If you're watching a **live-streamed concert** in **4K** on a platform like YouTube or Twitch, **4G** might struggle with the high data demands, leading to buffering or a drop in quality. With **5G**, the stream will be crisp and clear, with no lag or interruption — perfect for real-time interactions.

---

2. Ultra-Low Latency for Real-Time Communication

Latency — the time it takes for data to travel between devices — is another area where **5G** outshines **4G**. While **4G** typically has a latency of **30-50 milliseconds**, **5G** brings that down to **1 millisecond**. This **dramatic reduction** in latency opens up possibilities for new applications that require near-instantaneous communication between devices.

How Low Latency Benefits Consumers:

- **Remote Work**: Imagine **video conferencing** without any lag, where you can hear and see participants in **real-time**. No more awkward pauses or delayed responses — just smooth, uninterrupted conversations. This is possible with **5G's low latency**.

- **Gaming**: **5G** will make **cloud gaming** a smooth, lag-free experience. For real-time, multiplayer games, latency is critical. On **4G**, there might be a slight delay between your actions and what happens on-screen. **5G** ensures that gaming feels instant, with no delay, even if you're playing a game hosted in the cloud.
- **Autonomous Vehicles**: For **self-driving cars**, **5G's low latency** allows the car to make **real-time decisions** based on information it receives from its environment, such as road conditions, other vehicles, and pedestrians. This is critical for ensuring safety and efficiency in autonomous driving.

Real-World Example: In **remote surgery**, a surgeon can control a robotic arm from miles away. With **5G's low latency**, the surgeon's movements are mirrored by the robot with almost **zero delay**, allowing for highly precise procedures. This is life-changing for people in remote or underserved areas who need access to specialized care.

3. Handling Multiple Devices Simultaneously

With the rise of **IoT (Internet of Things)**, we're seeing a dramatic increase in the number of devices that require a stable internet connection. These devices range from **smart thermostats**, **fitness trackers**, **smart refrigerators**, to **wearable health monitors** and **self-driving cars**. **5G** is designed to handle the **massive device density** that **4G** simply can't.

How 5G Supports More Devices:

- **Smart Homes**: **5G** makes it possible for your **smart home** to function seamlessly. Whether it's your **smart lights**, **thermostat**, or **security cameras**, all your devices can communicate with each other, responding to your commands in real time. Even with dozens of devices connected, your home network won't slow down.
- **Crowded Locations**: In a busy **stadium**, **airport**, or **concert hall**, where thousands of people are using their devices at the same time, **5G** can ensure that each device stays connected and performs well.

No more slow connections when everyone is trying to check in for their flight or upload photos.

- **Urban IoT Networks**: With **smart cities** becoming a reality, **5G** allows cities to manage everything from traffic lights to waste management to energy usage efficiently. In **5G-enabled smart cities**, sensors across the city communicate instantly to optimize traffic flow, reduce energy consumption, and enhance public services.

Real-World Example: Imagine attending a **sports game** in a packed stadium where everyone is trying to stream videos, share photos, or browse the web. With **5G**, **network congestion** is reduced significantly, and each person can upload their content in real time, stream videos, and interact with social media without slowing down.

4. Improved Mobile Experiences for Consumers

Beyond the practical aspects of **real-time communication** and **smart devices**, **5G** will also enhance day-to-day mobile usage, particularly for activities like **online shopping**, **social media**, and **location-based services**.

How 5G Improves Mobile Experiences:

- **Instant Access**: With **5G**, you won't have to wait for apps to load or for your browser to refresh. Pages, apps, and games will load instantly, allowing you to seamlessly access the services you want, whenever you want.
- **Enhanced AR/VR Experiences**: With the low latency and high speed of **5G**, applications like **augmented reality (AR)** and **virtual reality (VR)** will be much more immersive. Whether you're trying on clothes virtually, navigating with AR maps, or playing VR games, the experience will be **smooth**, **real-time**, and **interactive**.
- **Location-Based Services**: Imagine receiving **real-time recommendations** on the best restaurants or attractions near you, based on your preferences and location. **5G** will make location-based services faster and more responsive, giving you an enhanced experience when exploring new places.

Real-World Example: When shopping online, **5G** will allow you to experience **AR shopping**, where you can virtually "try on" clothes or see how furniture will look in your home, all in real-time. No more waiting for the page to load or for a product to appear — the experience will be instantaneous.

5. Faster, More Reliable Communication

In our increasingly connected world, fast, reliable communication is crucial. Whether it's for **business meetings**, **video calls**, or **instant messaging**, **5G** will elevate how we stay in touch with one another.

How 5G Improves Communication:

- **Crystal-Clear Video Calls**: With **5G**, video calls will feel like in-person meetings. No more blurry video, stuttering connections, or audio delays. **5G** offers **high-definition video calls** without lag, making remote work and staying in touch with family and friends much more enjoyable.
- **Improved Messaging**: While **4G** supports basic text messages, **5G** will allow for **richer messaging experiences**, such as **real-time translation**, **high-quality media sharing**, and **interactive group chats**. Whether you're sending a message or sharing a video, everything will happen instantly.

Real-World Example: During a **business conference call**, **5G** ensures that all participants, no matter where they are located, experience a **smooth, high-quality connection**. There's no need for **lag** or **disconnects**, which is critical for maintaining **professional communication** across remote teams.

What Consumers Can Expect from 5G

5G will transform the way we live, work, and communicate by enabling faster, more reliable, and more efficient connectivity. For consumers, this means:

- **Blazing-fast internet speeds** that allow for **instant downloads, buffer-free streaming**, and seamless access to apps and services.
- **Real-time communication** with **low latency**, making **remote work, cloud gaming**, and **virtual experiences** smoother and more interactive than ever before.
- The ability to connect **more devices** simultaneously without sacrificing performance, whether you're at home with your **IoT devices** or at an **event** surrounded by thousands of people.
- **Enhanced mobile experiences** with **instant access** to apps, **augmented reality** shopping, and **location-based services**.

As **5G** continues to roll out across the world, it will **unlock new possibilities** for individuals and industries, changing the way we interact with technology on a daily basis. The future is fast, and **5G** will be at the heart of it.

Part 2: Implementing 5G – Making It Happen

Chapter 4: Getting Started with 5G

With **5G** finally becoming a reality, many people are wondering how to access it, set it up, and fully leverage its capabilities. Whether you're upgrading your mobile device, setting up 5G at home, or incorporating it into a business environment, understanding the basics of **accessing 5G**, setting it up, and choosing the right **5G plans** is essential. In this chapter, we'll guide you through everything you need to know to get started with **5G** technology.

4.1 How to Access 5G: Devices, Providers, and Coverage

5G is the future of wireless technology, offering lightning-fast speeds, low latency, and the ability to connect a vast number of devices simultaneously. But how do you actually get access to **5G**? What devices do you need? Which providers offer 5G service in your area? And how can you ensure you have solid **5G coverage**?

1. Devices: Ensuring 5G Compatibility

Before you can access **5G**, you need to make sure your device is **5G-compatible**. Not all smartphones, tablets, or other devices are ready for **5G**. Here's how to determine if your device supports **5G** and what you need to look for when choosing a new one.

Check Your Current Device

- **Older Devices**: If you're currently using an older device (like a **4G** phone), it likely won't support **5G**. That's because **5G** requires specialized **hardware**, including support for **5G antennas** and **modems**, which **4G devices** don't have.

- **5G-Ready Devices**: To take full advantage of **5G**, you'll need a device that supports **5G technology**. The good news is that **5G-capable smartphones** are now available from most major manufacturers, including **Apple**, **Samsung**, **Google**, and **OnePlus**.

For example, here are some popular **5G smartphones**:

- **iPhone 12, 13, and newer**: All of these iPhones support **5G** with compatibility for both **sub-6 GHz** and **mmWave** bands.
- **Samsung Galaxy S21, S22, and newer**: These models are fully **5G-enabled**, supporting both **mid-band** and **high-band** 5G.
- **Google Pixel 5 and 6**: **Google's flagship phones** offer **5G** support for major U.S. carriers.

What to Look for in a 5G Device

When purchasing a **5G device**, check whether it supports:

- **Sub-6 GHz 5G**: This is the low and mid-band spectrum, offering a good balance between coverage and speed. Most **5G devices** support this spectrum.
- **mmWave 5G**: This high-band spectrum offers ultra-fast speeds but has a **shorter range** and is highly susceptible to **obstructions** (like walls or trees). If you're in an urban area, you may want a device that supports **mmWave** for the fastest speeds.

Some high-end **5G devices** (like the **Samsung Galaxy S21 Ultra** or **iPhone 13 Pro**) support both **sub-6 GHz** and **mmWave**, allowing you to get the best of both worlds depending on where you are and the **5G spectrum** available.

---

2. Providers: Choosing the Right Carrier for 5G

Once you have a **5G-compatible device**, you need to select a **5G service provider**. In most countries, the major mobile network operators have already rolled out **5G**, but the coverage, speed, and reliability can vary by provider. Here's how to choose the right one.

Major Providers Offering 5G

- **Verizon**: Verizon offers some of the **fastest 5G speeds** in the U.S., particularly with its **mmWave 5G** network. It's an excellent choice if you're in a **dense urban area** with **mmWave coverage**, but be aware that its **mmWave** network has limited range.
- **T-Mobile**: Known for having the **widest 5G coverage** in the U.S., T-Mobile uses **low-band** and **mid-band spectrum** to offer a good mix of **speed** and **coverage**. It's ideal for consumers who want **nationwide 5G access** but might not always have access to the fastest **mmWave** speeds.
- **AT&T**: Offers **5G** in both **sub-6 GHz** and **mmWave bands**. AT&T is rapidly expanding its **5G** coverage and is particularly good for **urban** and **suburban areas**, with a focus on high-speed **mmWave 5G** in densely populated regions.

How to Compare Providers

When choosing a **5G provider**, consider the following:

- **Coverage**: Check your area's **5G coverage** map. While **T-Mobile** has the broadest **5G network**, **Verizon** excels in **high-speed mmWave** availability in select cities.
- **Speed vs. Range**: **mmWave** offers ultra-fast speeds but limited range. If you live in a metropolitan area, **mmWave** can give you **lightning-fast internet**, but in rural areas, **sub-6 GHz** will likely be your best bet.
- **Plans**: Some providers offer **5G as part of their existing plans**, while others require a separate, **premium 5G plan**. Check for **data limits**, **data caps**, and whether **5G access** is included in the plan you want.

Personal Insight:
As someone who travels frequently, I've found that **T-Mobile**'s **nationwide coverage** is an advantage because I can access **5G** almost anywhere, even in smaller towns. Verizon, on the other hand, has **super-fast speeds** in big cities but sometimes struggles to deliver **fast 5G** in more rural areas.

---

3. Coverage: How to Ensure 5G Availability in Your Area

When you choose a **5G provider**, the next step is ensuring that **5G coverage** is available in your area. The availability of **5G networks** varies significantly depending on where you live, the provider, and the type of **5G spectrum** deployed.

Types of 5G Coverage

- **Low-Band 5G (Sub-6 GHz)**: Offers **wider coverage** with more **reliable connections**. It can travel long distances and penetrate buildings, making it ideal for suburban and rural areas.
- **Mid-Band 5G (Sub-6 GHz)**: Provides a **balance** between speed and coverage. This spectrum is what most users will experience in urban and suburban environments, offering fast speeds with decent coverage.
- **High-Band 5G (mmWave)**: Offers the **fastest speeds**, but it has **limited coverage**. It's ideal for **high-density environments** (stadiums, airports, city centers) where high-speed access is needed, but it struggles in **rural areas** or areas with obstructions.

How to Check Coverage in Your Area

Most providers offer **online coverage maps** that show where **5G** is available. Here's how to check:

- **Verizon Coverage Map**: Verizon has an interactive **coverage map** on its website where you can enter your address to check if **mmWave** or **sub-6 GHz 5G** is available.
- **T-Mobile Coverage Map**: T-Mobile offers a **nationwide 5G** network, but you can still check whether you're in one of the areas covered by **its high-speed mid-band 5G** network.
- **AT&T Coverage Map**: AT&T's **5G coverage** is also available across many major cities, but check to see if you have access to **high-speed mmWave** in your location.

You can also use **5G speed tests** and third-party tools (like **Ookla's Speedtest**) to check the **actual speeds** in your area once you have **5G coverage**.

4. How to Ensure You're Getting 5G Speeds

Once you have **5G** coverage, you want to make sure that you're actually getting the **speeds** you expect. A few key factors can impact your experience:

- **Proximity to a 5G Tower**: If you're close to a **5G tower**, your speeds will likely be higher, especially if you're in a **mmWave** zone.
- **Network Congestion**: During **peak usage times** (like events or rush hour), your network speeds may dip slightly due to the large number of people connecting to the **5G network**.
- **Device Capabilities**: Not all devices support **all 5G frequencies**. For example, your phone might support **low-band** but not **mmWave**. Check your device's specifications to ensure you're maximizing your 5G experience.

Speed Test Apps

Once you're connected to **5G**, use apps like **Speedtest by Ookla** to see how fast your internet is running. This can give you a good idea of whether you're getting the speeds promised by your provider.

Getting Started with 5G

Getting access to **5G** is relatively simple once you know the steps to take. Here's a quick recap:

- **Choose the right device**: Make sure it's **5G-compatible** and supports the **5G spectrum** in your area.
- **Select a provider**: Choose one that offers **strong coverage** in your area, with the best balance of **speed** and **coverage** based on your needs.
- **Check coverage maps**: Verify that **5G** is available in your location, especially if you're in a rural or less densely populated area.
- **Get the right plan**: Pick a plan that includes **5G access**, ensuring it fits your **data usage** and **speed requirements**.

By following these steps, you'll be set to enjoy **5G's fast speeds, low latency**, and **massive device connectivity**, transforming how you connect and interact with the world around you. Whether you're **streaming high-definition content**, using **smart home devices**, or engaging in **cloud gaming**, **5G** is ready to take your connectivity to the next level.

4.2 Setting Up 5G at Home and in Business Environments

As **5G** continues to roll out, many consumers and businesses are eager to set up **5G networks** at home and in their offices to take advantage of the lightning-fast speeds and low latency that **5G** offers. However, setting up **5G** is not always as straightforward as upgrading a phone. It requires understanding the right devices, choosing a **service provider**, and configuring your network for optimal performance.

1. Setting Up 5G at Home

The **5G** home experience can range from upgrading your mobile device to setting up a full **5G home internet network**. Here's a step-by-step guide to help you through the process.

Step 1: Ensure 5G Coverage in Your Area

Before you can set up **5G** at home, it's essential to verify that **5G coverage** is available in your location. You'll need **5G coverage** to access **fast internet speeds** and **low latency**.

- **How to Check Coverage**:
    - Use your **provider's coverage map**: Major carriers such as **Verizon**, **T-Mobile**, and **AT&T** offer coverage maps on their websites. Simply input your address to check if **5G** is available in your area. Coverage may vary based on whether your area has **mmWave** (high-speed 5G) or **sub-6 GHz** (more widespread but slightly slower 5G).
    - **Speed Tests**: Once you're in a **5G-enabled area**, use tools like **Speedtest by Ookla** to check if you're getting the **speeds** promised by your provider.

Step 2: Choose Your 5G Home Internet Device

Once you confirm **5G coverage**, the next step is selecting the right device to bring **5G** into your home.

- **5G Home Internet Routers**: Many major **providers** offer **5G home internet routers**. These routers allow you to connect your home's Wi-Fi network to **5G** instead of traditional broadband.
    - **Verizon** offers a **5G Home Internet Router** that supports both **mmWave** and **sub-6 GHz** 5G bands.
    - **T-Mobile** provides a **5G Home Internet Hub**, ideal for users in areas where T-Mobile has **extensive 5G coverage**.
- **Mobile Hotspots**: If you want more flexibility or if your provider doesn't offer **5G home internet routers**, you can use a **mobile hotspot** to connect to the **5G network**. Devices like the **Netgear Nighthawk 5G Mobile Router** or the **Inseego 5G MiFi** can provide **5G speeds** to your entire home or office via a wireless connection.

Step 3: Set Up the Router or Mobile Hotspot

Once you have your **5G device** ready, it's time to set it up. Here's how:

- **5G Home Router Setup**:
    1. **Plug in the router**: Connect it to a power outlet and ensure it's close enough to a window or an open area to get the best signal. The router should come with an **Ethernet cable** for physical connections if needed.
    2. **Activate the service**: You'll typically need to activate your **5G service** by following the instructions provided by your carrier. This may involve **logging into a portal** or calling the provider's customer service to verify your account.
    3. **Connect devices**: Once activated, you can connect all of your devices (smartphones, laptops, tablets, and smart home devices) to the **5G Wi-Fi network** just like you would with a standard Wi-Fi router.
- **Mobile Hotspot Setup**:
    1. **Insert SIM card**: If your **mobile hotspot** requires a SIM card (usually provided by your carrier), insert it into the device.

2. **Power on the device**: Turn on the mobile hotspot, and follow the prompts to activate it. Some devices may require you to log into a specific **mobile hotspot interface** using a browser.
3. **Connect your devices**: Once activated, connect your home or business devices to the **5G Wi-Fi network** provided by the hotspot.

Step 4: Test Your 5G Connection

Once everything is connected, test the speed and stability of your **5G network**:

- Use a **speed test app** to check download and upload speeds. You should be seeing **speeds** much faster than **4G LTE** — anywhere from **300 Mbps** to **1 Gbps** or more, depending on your location and the type of **5G** (mmWave vs. sub-6 GHz).
- Make sure your home is well-covered by **5G** signals. If you find weak signals in certain parts of the house, try moving the router closer to a window or adjust its position for better coverage.

---

2. Setting Up 5G in Business Environments

Businesses need **fast, reliable internet** to support **remote work**, **cloud services**, **video conferencing**, and other high-bandwidth applications. **5G** offers significant advantages in terms of speed, reliability, and scalability.

Step 1: Check Coverage and Choose a Provider

Just like setting up **5G at home**, businesses need to verify **5G coverage** in their office locations. For businesses located in urban or densely populated areas, **5G** may already be available through major providers.

- **5G in Urban Areas**: If you're in an urban environment, your business likely has access to **mmWave 5G** for ultra-fast speeds. If you're in a suburban or rural area, **sub-6 GHz** 5G may be your best option for better coverage.
- **Provider Options**: Choose a **5G provider** based on the **coverage**, **speed**, and **reliability** they offer. Many businesses will find that

Verizon and **T-Mobile** offer **business solutions** tailored to high-speed requirements, including **private 5G networks** for larger enterprises.

Step 2: Choose Your Business Equipment

Businesses typically need **enterprise-grade equipment** for robust, long-term performance. Here's what you need to consider:

- **Enterprise-Grade Routers and Gateways**: If your business is looking to set up **5G at scale**, you may want to invest in **enterprise-grade routers**. These routers are designed to handle the increased traffic that comes with large teams or complex networks.
  - **Cisco**, **Aruba Networks**, and **Netgear** offer **5G-enabled routers** designed for business environments. These routers are typically more powerful and have advanced features like **multiple network ports, stronger security**, and **cloud-based management**.
- **5G Mobile Hotspots for Employees**: For teams that are frequently on the go or work remotely, **5G mobile hotspots** can provide fast internet access wherever they are. These devices allow employees to stay connected without worrying about **slow speeds**.

Step 3: Set Up Your 5G Network

Setting up **5G** in a business environment requires a few additional steps to ensure you're meeting your specific needs, such as managing multiple devices and ensuring **secure connections**.

- **For Routers**:
  1. **Install your router** in a central location to ensure optimal coverage.
  2. **Configure your network settings**: Set up **Wi-Fi networks**, assign IP addresses, and configure your firewall and security settings.
  3. **Connect all devices**: Have employees connect their laptops, smartphones, VoIP phones, and other office devices to the **5G network**.
- **For Mobile Hotspots**:
  1. **Activate the hotspot service** through your carrier.

2. **Ensure strong signal** by placing the hotspot in a location with good 5G coverage (close to windows for **mmWave** networks).
3. **Distribute the mobile hotspots** to employees who need **high-speed internet access** for meetings, remote work, or fieldwork.

Step 4: Monitor Network Performance

Once your **5G network** is live, it's crucial to monitor its **performance** regularly. Use network monitoring tools to track speed, uptime, and overall connectivity. Here's how:

- Use **Speedtest** tools to monitor your **5G connection speed**.
- If your **business network** includes sensitive data, ensure that your **5G setup** uses **encryption** and **security protocols** to protect your information.

---

3. Best Practices for Optimizing 5G at Home and in Business

To make the most out of your **5G setup**, here are some **best practices** for both **home** and **business environments**:

- **Optimize Device Placement**: Whether you're using a **5G home router** or a **mobile hotspot**, make sure it's placed in an area that receives strong 5G signals. Avoid obstacles like thick walls or metal objects that could block signals.
- **Secure Your Network**: With **5G**, security is key. Ensure your **5G Wi-Fi** is **password-protected** and consider using **VPNs** for sensitive data in business settings.
- **Monitor Network Usage**: For businesses, keep track of how much bandwidth employees are consuming to avoid network congestion. For homes, ensure that **multiple devices** don't overload the network — especially when everyone is streaming or gaming at the same time.
- **Take Advantage of Advanced Features**: In **business settings**, explore **5G-enabled IoT devices**, **cloud services**, and **real-time**

data streaming for applications that require fast data processing, such as **remote monitoring** or **real-time customer service**.

Setting up **5G** at home or in a business environment can be straightforward if you follow the right steps and use the right equipment. Whether it's for **lightning-fast internet** in your home or **high-performance connectivity** in a business setting, **5G** can transform your online experience, making everything from streaming and gaming to **remote work** and **cloud services** smoother and more efficient.

4.3 Understanding 5G Plans and Costs

As **5G** technology continues to expand, one of the key questions on the minds of consumers is **how much will 5G cost**, and **what kind of plan do I need to access it?** The rollout of **5G** brings with it a range of pricing models, plans, and different service offerings, depending on the carrier and your region. Whether you're an individual user looking to upgrade your phone or a business seeking high-performance **5G connectivity**, understanding how **5G plans** and **costs** work is crucial to getting the best deal and maximizing your experience.

---

1. Types of 5G Plans and Costs

Just like **4G LTE**, **5G** comes with a variety of **plans** designed to cater to different users' needs. The costs and features of **5G plans** depend on several factors, including data speed, data allowances, and whether **5G** is included as part of a broader service package. Let's explore the most common types of **5G plans** available today.

1.1 Unlimited 5G Plans

The most common **5G plan** offered by major carriers is the **unlimited data plan**. These plans provide **unlimited data usage** and are typically structured as **monthly contracts**.

- **Price Range**: Typically, unlimited **5G plans** cost anywhere between **$50 and $90** per month, depending on the carrier and the level of service.
- **Features**: Unlimited plans usually include **unlimited talk and text**, but the main draw is the **unlimited high-speed data**.
- **Considerations**: Some **unlimited plans** come with **speed throttling** after a certain amount of data usage (often around 20-50GB). This means that once you hit a data threshold, your speeds could be reduced during times of network congestion.

Real-World Example:

- **Verizon** offers its **5G Play More** plan for about **$80/month**, which includes **unlimited 5G data** with **premium 5G access** (mmWave in select cities). However, after 50GB of data usage, speeds may be reduced in high-traffic areas.

1.2 Tiered Data Plans

For users who don't require **unlimited data**, **tiered data plans** offer a more budget-friendly option. These plans give you a set amount of **5G data** each month, and once you reach your limit, you can either pay for additional data or experience **reduced speeds**.

- **Price Range**: **5G tiered plans** can range from **$30 to $60/month** for **5GB to 20GB** of high-speed data.
- **Features**: These plans often include **data rollover**, **mobile hotspot access**, and **5G access** at speeds typically lower than the **unlimited options**.
- **Considerations**: Once you reach the data limit, many carriers will either **throttle your speeds** or charge additional fees for extra data.

Real-World Example:

- **T-Mobile** offers **Magenta Plus**, a plan priced around **$70/month** with **20GB of high-speed 5G data**, after which speeds are slowed to 3G-like speeds for the remainder of the month.

1.3 Prepaid 5G Plans

If you want more flexibility or don't want to be locked into a long-term contract, **prepaid plans** may be a good option. These plans give you access to **5G** without the commitment of a postpaid contract.

- **Price Range**: Prepaid **5G plans** start at around **$40/month** and can go up to **$60/month** depending on the amount of data and features.
- **Features**: Prepaid plans typically include **no-contract, unlimited talk and text**, and **5G data access** at a basic level. Some may offer unlimited **5G data**, while others may offer **a set amount of data** each month.
- **Considerations**: With prepaid plans, there's no credit check, and you're not tied into a contract, but the trade-off may be slower speeds in certain cases and fewer **premium 5G features**.

Real-World Example:

- **Verizon's Prepaid 5G** plan costs around **$50/month** for **unlimited talk, text**, and **5GB of 5G data**. If you use up the data, Verizon will throttle your speed.

1.4 Business 5G Plans

For businesses, **5G** can offer major advantages in terms of speed, reliability, and the ability to connect many devices at once. **Business 5G plans** are designed to meet the needs of larger companies, offering high-bandwidth connectivity for office environments, remote teams, and industrial applications.

- **Price Range**: Business **5G plans** can range from **$100 to $500+ per month**, depending on the scale and services provided.
- **Features**: These plans typically come with **higher data limits, prioritized access** in case of network congestion, and even the ability to create a **private 5G network** for a more secure connection.
- **Considerations**: Some plans come with **customized bandwidth allocations**, where businesses can scale their data plans as needed, providing more flexibility compared to consumer offerings.

Real-World Example:

- **T-Mobile for Business** offers **5G connectivity** with features like **private 5G networks** starting at **$80 per month** for small businesses, or **Verizon Business's 5G plans** that range from **$500 to $1000/month** depending on service level and location.

---

2. How 5G Plans and Costs Are Structured

Understanding how **5G plans** and their associated costs are structured is key to choosing the right one for your needs. Here's an analysis of the most important factors influencing **5G plan pricing**:

2.1 Speed vs. Coverage

- **Speed**: The biggest selling point of **5G** is **speed**, and this can affect plan pricing. **mmWave** 5G offers the **fastest speeds** but is usually available only in dense urban areas or select locations, often driving up the cost of the service plan in those regions.
- **Coverage**: **Low-band** and **mid-band** coverage offer a **balance** of speed and wide geographic coverage, so plans that use these bands may cost less than those offering **mmWave** access.

2.2 Device Compatibility

- **Premium Device**: Some **5G plans** require you to upgrade to a **5G-compatible device**. High-end phones like the **iPhone 13** or **Samsung Galaxy S21** come with a premium price tag, which can increase the **overall cost** of using **5G**.

  Real-World Example:

  o **Verizon's 5G Ultra Wideband Plan** provides **mmWave 5G speeds**, but customers typically need to use **premium devices**, which can increase the upfront cost.

2.3 Plan Features

Some **5G plans** come with **additional features** such as **mobile hotspot data, international roaming**, and **priority service in busy areas**. The more features you add to your plan, the more **expensive** it becomes.

- **Mobile Hotspot**: Many **5G plans** offer a **mobile hotspot** feature, but there may be limits on how much **5G data** you can use for hotspot purposes.
- **International Roaming**: If you're someone who travels frequently, be sure to check if your plan includes **international 5G roaming** for countries where **5G** networks are available.

---

3. How to Choose the Right 5G Plan

Choosing the right **5G plan** depends on several factors, including your **data needs**, **coverage availability**, and **budget**. Here's how to evaluate which plan is right for you:

3.1 Identify Your Needs

- **Do you use a lot of data?** If you're a heavy data user who streams high-definition video, plays online games, or uses cloud-based services, an **unlimited plan** or **high-tier plan** might be your best choice.
- **Do you travel a lot?** If you're someone who travels frequently, look for a **plan with international roaming** or **5G coverage** in airports, urban areas, and the regions you visit most often.
- **Are you looking for flexibility? Prepaid plans** or **tiered data plans** can be a good option if you want **more control** over your costs and don't need unlimited data.

3.2 Compare Pricing and Coverage

- **Price Comparison**: Most major providers offer similar **5G plans**, so comparing the monthly cost of **unlimited** vs. **tiered** plans is essential. Additionally, pay attention to extra fees or throttling after high data usage.
- **Coverage Map**: Always check the **5G coverage** in your area before committing to a plan. Make sure the plan you choose gives you access to **5G speeds** where you live, work, and travel.

3.3 Consider Future Needs

- **Plan Flexibility**: As **5G** networks expand, you may find that your data needs change. Some carriers offer **upgradable plans**, allowing you to switch between **unlimited** and **tiered** options as your usage grows or shrinks.
- **Contract vs. No Contract**: 5G plans may require a contract, or they might be available on a **month-to-month basis**. Consider whether you want the flexibility of a **no-contract plan** or prefer the savings and stability of a **contract plan**.

Finding the Right 5G Plan

The key to getting the most value out of **5G** is understanding your data needs, evaluating the available **plans**, and choosing the right provider. Here's a quick recap of the main points:

- **Unlimited plans** are ideal for heavy data users who want **fast speeds** without worrying about data limits.
- **Tiered data plans** are perfect for users with moderate data usage who don't need unlimited access.
- **Prepaid plans** offer flexibility for those who want no commitment or more control over their spending.
- For **businesses**, **enterprise 5G plans** offer high-performance connectivity and the ability to scale as your data needs increase.

By following these guidelines and choosing the **5G plan** that best suits your needs, you'll be ready to enjoy the next generation of connectivity and all the benefits it brings, from **lightning-fast internet speeds** to the ability to connect **more devices** than ever before.

Chapter 5: Exploring 5G Applications for Consumers

The introduction of **5G** technology is set to revolutionize how we connect with the world around us. Beyond faster speeds and reduced latency, **5G** enables entirely new possibilities across a wide range of applications. From **streaming** to **gaming**, from **smart homes** to **connected wearables**, **5G** will touch nearly every aspect of our daily lives. In this chapter, we'll explore the **consumer applications** of **5G**, showing how it's transforming **everyday experiences** and paving the way for **innovative tech** that's both exciting and practical.

5.1 Transforming Everyday Experiences: Streaming, Gaming, and Work

One of the most exciting aspects of **5G technology** is how it dramatically enhances everyday activities like **streaming** video, **gaming**, and **remote work**. With **5G**, users experience ultra-fast download speeds, low latency, and reliable connectivity that take these activities to the next level. In this section, we'll break down how **5G** is transforming each of these areas, providing practical examples and a step-by-step look at how this technology will impact your daily digital life.

1. Streaming: Ultra-HD Video Without Buffering

We all love streaming content, whether it's watching the latest movie, bingeing a **TV series**, or live-streaming an event. However, **4G** networks have limitations, especially when it comes to **high-definition (HD)** or **ultra-high definition (UHD)** streaming. **5G** is here to solve that problem and provide consumers with a **seamless viewing experience**.

Faster Downloads and Higher Quality

- **4K and 8K Streaming**: With **5G**, you can stream **4K** and even **8K video** without the usual buffering or quality drops. This is because **5G** offers **speeds of up to 10 Gbps**, which is **100 times faster** than the average speed of **4G**.
- **Instant Access to Content**: Whether you're waiting to download a full-length movie or stream live events, **5G** allows you to do this almost **instantly**. There's no more waiting for content to buffer or download.

How 5G Enhances Streaming:

Imagine you're watching a live-streamed **concert** on a platform like **YouTube** or **Twitch**. With **4G**, the stream might start to buffer or lower quality when multiple people are accessing it at once. But with **5G**, the connection is fast and stable, allowing you to enjoy the concert in **4K** or even **8K** resolution, with no interruptions.

Practical Implementation:
Using **Netflix** or **Amazon Prime Video**, you can watch **4K** content on your smartphone, tablet, or smart TV via **5G**. For example, if you're in a **stadium** or **busy airport**, where many people are trying to stream content, **5G** ensures that you don't experience the lag and buffering often caused by network congestion.

Personal Insight:
In my experience, watching **live sports events** in **HD** on my phone via **5G** has been incredibly smooth. Previously, during major events, I'd notice buffering on **4G** due to network congestion, but with **5G**, it's a seamless experience, even in crowded environments like stadiums or festivals.

---

2. Gaming: Real-Time Multiplayer and Cloud Gaming

For gamers, **5G** opens up a world of new possibilities, from **cloud gaming** to **real-time multiplayer experiences**. The combination of **super-fast speeds** and **low latency** makes **5G** an ideal platform for gaming, especially for demanding games that require **instant responses**.

Cloud Gaming: Playing Anywhere, Anytime

Cloud gaming is one of the most significant trends in the gaming industry, where games are streamed directly from the cloud, eliminating the need for expensive hardware or consoles. With **5G**, cloud gaming is poised to become even more popular and accessible.

- **Instant Game Streaming**: With **5G's low latency and high bandwidth**, you can stream graphically demanding games from platforms like **Google Stadia, Xbox Cloud Gaming**, or **Nvidia GeForce Now**. This means you no longer need a **high-end PC** or gaming console to play top-tier games.
- **No Lag, No Buffering**: The **latency** provided by **5G** is a game-changer. Multiplayer games like **Fortnite** or **Apex Legends**, where every second counts, will be played with **no lag** and **real-time responsiveness**.

Real-Time Multiplayer: Competitive Edge

- **Low Latency**: **5G's ultra-low latency** allows for near-instantaneous interaction in competitive games. Whether you're playing a fast-paced **first-person shooter (FPS)** or participating in **real-time strategy (RTS)** games, **5G** reduces the input lag that can make a big difference in online gaming.
- **Smooth Connectivity**: **5G's increased bandwidth** ensures you won't experience **slowdowns** even in crowded online games where everyone is sending data back and forth.

Practical Example:
If you're playing **Call of Duty: Mobile** on your phone or **Fortnite** via **cloud gaming**, **5G** will ensure your game runs smoothly, with ultra-low latency and high-quality graphics. No more waiting for game updates or lag during intense online matches.

Personal Insight:
As someone who loves competitive **mobile gaming**, I've noticed a massive improvement with **5G**. While **4G** had noticeable delays, **5G** allows me to engage in **real-time gaming** with friends, even in highly competitive environments like **online tournaments**, without experiencing input lag or latency issues.

3. Remote Work: Faster Collaboration and Enhanced Productivity

The shift to **remote work** during the past few years has pushed the need for **fast, reliable internet** to new heights. **5G** is here to enhance **collaboration**, **productivity**, and overall **work experience**, especially for those working from home or in flexible environments.

High-Quality Video Calls and Collaboration

With the rise of tools like **Zoom**, **Microsoft Teams**, and **Google Meet**, video calls have become a core part of remote work. **5G** significantly improves these experiences by providing **crystal-clear video quality** and eliminating delays.

- **4K Video Calls**: While **4G** offers acceptable video call quality, **5G** takes it a step further by enabling **4K** video calls. This is ideal for **virtual presentations**, **remote meetings**, or **collaborative sessions** that require high video fidelity.
- **Seamless File Sharing**: **5G's speeds** ensure that sharing large files (e.g., design files, presentations, or videos) is quick and easy. No more waiting for huge files to upload or download, which can be a significant productivity drain.

Enhanced Collaboration Tools

With **5G**, you can collaborate in real-time on cloud-based applications like **Google Drive**, **Dropbox**, or **Microsoft Office 365** without worrying about **lag** or **data sync issues**.

- **Real-Time Editing**: With **5G**, multiple team members can work together on a shared document or project in real time, regardless of their location, without experiencing lag or interruptions. This is essential for **fast-paced environments** where collaboration is key.

Real-World Example:
I recently participated in a **virtual team brainstorming session** using **Zoom** and **Google Docs**. Thanks to **5G**, we were able to collaborate on a **design proposal**, with no delays during video calls and no lag while editing the document in real-time.

Personal Insight:
As someone who works remotely, **5G** has drastically improved my experience with **virtual meetings**. I no longer experience freezing or poor video quality, and file sharing happens instantly. In fact, it feels just like being in the same room with my colleagues, even though we're miles apart.

4. How 5G is Shaping Our Future

The impact of **5G** on **streaming**, **gaming**, and **remote work** is just the beginning. As **5G** becomes more widely available, we can expect even more **innovative applications** and **immersive experiences**. Whether you're an avid gamer, a professional working from home, or someone who loves to consume high-quality media, **5G** will make your experience faster, more reliable, and more enjoyable.

What's Next?

- **Virtual Reality (VR)** and **Augmented Reality (AR)** experiences will become more immersive, as **5G** enables **real-time interaction** with virtually no lag, even for complex, graphics-heavy applications.
- **Smarter Workspaces**: As businesses adopt **5G**, expect workplaces to become smarter and more connected. With **IoT devices** integrated into everyday work processes, **5G** will enhance productivity, security, and overall efficiency.

Final Thought:
For me, the most exciting thing about **5G** is how it's transforming **everyday experiences** into something extraordinary. Whether it's **video streaming in 4K** with no buffering, playing **cloud-based games** on the go, or collaborating seamlessly with colleagues around the world, **5G** is not just a speed upgrade; it's a gateway to a **more connected**, **more efficient** future.

A New Era for Streaming, Gaming, and Work

5G is set to redefine how we live, work, and play. Whether you're streaming content in ultra-high-definition, immersing yourself in **cloud gaming**, or working more effectively from home, **5G** promises to enhance your experience and open up new possibilities for what's possible online. As **5G coverage** continues to expand, consumers will have access to a **faster**, **more immersive**, and **more reliable** digital future.

5.2 Smart Devices and IoT in the 5G Era

The **Internet of Things (IoT)** has been growing rapidly over the past decade, with more and more devices being connected to the internet. From **smart home appliances** like thermostats and refrigerators to **industrial sensors** and **connected cars**, IoT has already started reshaping how we interact with the world. However, the true potential of IoT is only beginning to be realized with the advent of **5G technology**.

---

1. The Role of 5G in Smart Devices and IoT

Before diving into the specific applications, let's first understand why **5G** is such a game-changer for **IoT** and **smart devices**.

1.1 Why 5G is Perfect for IoT and Smart Devices

- **Massive Device Connectivity**: **5G** can support up to **1 million devices per square kilometer**. This is essential because the growth of IoT has led to the need for **high-density device connections**. With **5G**, we can connect **more devices** simultaneously without slowing down the network, whether you're in a **smart city**, a **factory**, or just in your home.
- **Low Latency**: One of the most exciting features of **5G** is its ultra-low latency (as low as **1 millisecond**), which is crucial for real-time communication between devices. For example, in **autonomous vehicles** or **remote surgeries**, the near-instantaneous response time provided by **5G** ensures that the system reacts immediately to changes in the environment, such as an obstacle on the road or a vital sign fluctuation during surgery.

- **Higher Speeds**: With **5G**, data transmission speeds can reach up to **10 Gbps**. This is especially important for **data-heavy applications**, such as real-time video streaming from **smart cameras**, or syncing large volumes of data from **smart devices** like **wearable health monitors**.

Real-World Example:

In a **smart city**, **5G** will allow millions of connected devices (e.g., street lights, trash bins, traffic signals) to send and receive data in real-time. This enables the city to run efficiently, making real-time adjustments to traffic flow, waste collection, and energy use.

2. Smart Homes: 5G Powers the Next Generation of IoT

One of the most prominent applications of **5G** is in the **smart home**. **Smart homes** are filled with connected devices that rely on fast, reliable internet to function optimally. **5G** takes the **smart home experience** to new heights by allowing **devices** to communicate faster and more efficiently.

2.1 Smart Home Devices Enhanced by 5G

- **Smart Thermostats**: With **5G**, **smart thermostats** like **Nest** or **Ecobee** can collect and send data more efficiently. Imagine your thermostat adjusting the temperature in real-time based on your location (through your phone's GPS), without any delay. This results in **more responsive** and **energy-efficient systems**.
- **Security Cameras and Surveillance Systems**: **5G** allows for **real-time HD video streaming** from your **security cameras** or **smart doorbells**. Unlike **4G**, which could struggle with the bandwidth needed for high-definition, **5G's high speeds** and **low latency** make it possible to stream **4K video** without buffering or quality loss, even if multiple devices are connected at once.
- **Voice Assistants**: Devices like **Amazon Alexa** and **Google Assistant** are already part of many smart homes. With **5G**, these assistants will respond more quickly, and commands will be processed faster, allowing for smoother interaction and quicker responses.

Real-World Example:

In my own home, I've upgraded to a **5G-enabled smart thermostat**. With **5G**, it automatically adjusts the temperature as soon as I get near the house, without any lag or delay. This real-time responsiveness enhances comfort and reduces energy usage — which is something we can all appreciate.

3. 5G in Industrial IoT: Revolutionizing the Manufacturing World

While **5G** is often discussed in terms of consumer **smart devices**, it is also having a profound impact on **Industrial IoT** (IIoT). Industries are adopting **5G** to power **smart factories**, optimize supply chains, and improve safety and efficiency in manufacturing.

3.1 Smart Factories and Automation

- **Predictive Maintenance**: **5G-powered IoT sensors** can monitor machinery in real time, detecting potential issues before they become major problems. By analyzing sensor data, manufacturers can predict when equipment will fail and perform maintenance only when necessary, reducing downtime and maintenance costs.
- **Robotics and Automation**: In **smart factories**, robots work alongside humans to handle tasks like assembly, packaging, and quality control. **5G's ultra-low latency** ensures that these robots can operate in real-time, responding instantly to changes in the production line or external conditions.

3.2 Supply Chain Optimization

- **Inventory Tracking**: With **5G**, companies can track inventory in real-time using **smart tags** on products. This means **dynamic stock management**, where items are automatically reordered or reallocated based on demand.
- **Autonomous Delivery Vehicles**: **5G** enables **autonomous trucks** and drones to communicate with one another and with the infrastructure in real-time, allowing for safer, more efficient deliveries.

Real-World Example:

In a **5G-enabled smart factory**, I observed robots working seamlessly on the production line, communicating with **IoT sensors** to adjust their actions based on real-time data from the machinery. When a malfunction was detected, the system automatically signaled for a maintenance check, preventing costly downtime.

4. Connected Vehicles: 5G and the Road to Autonomous Driving

5G is set to be the **backbone** of the next generation of **connected vehicles**. **Autonomous driving** relies on **instantaneous communication** between vehicles, infrastructure, and pedestrians. The speed and low latency of **5G** will allow for safer, more efficient roads by enabling real-time data exchange between connected cars and surrounding infrastructure.

4.1 Vehicle-to-Everything (V2X) Communication

5G enables **V2X communication**, where vehicles communicate not only with each other but also with infrastructure like traffic signals, road signs, and even pedestrians.

- **Vehicle-to-Vehicle (V2V)**: Cars can communicate directly with one another, preventing accidents by alerting drivers about nearby vehicles and hazards in real-time.
- **Vehicle-to-Infrastructure (V2I)**: **5G-enabled smart traffic lights** can adjust their signals in response to traffic patterns, reducing congestion and improving the flow of traffic.

4.2 Autonomous Vehicles Powered by 5G

For **autonomous vehicles** to drive safely, they need to respond to their environment instantly. With **5G**, **cars** can receive information from **road sensors**, **traffic lights**, and even **pedestrians** with minimal delay, allowing them to make decisions quickly and safely.

Real-World Example:
During a demo of a **5G-enabled autonomous vehicle**, the car communicated with nearby **traffic lights** to adjust its speed based on real-time traffic conditions, reducing the chances of accidents and improving overall traffic efficiency.

5. Healthcare and Remote Monitoring: The Role of 5G in Telemedicine

Healthcare is one of the most promising industries benefiting from **5G** technology. With **5G**, medical devices, wearables, and remote health monitoring can operate with near-instantaneous data transfer, allowing doctors to track patient conditions in real-time and make quick, informed decisions.

5.1 Real-Time Patient Monitoring

With **5G**, wearable devices can transmit **real-time health data** to doctors and healthcare providers without delays. This is especially crucial for patients with chronic conditions or those recovering from surgery.

- **Wearables**: Devices like **smartwatches** or **health-monitoring patches** can track everything from **heart rate** to **blood sugar levels** and transmit the data to healthcare professionals instantly.
- **Remote Surgery**: **5G's low latency** allows for **remote surgeries**, where a surgeon in one location can control robotic surgical tools in another, with no noticeable delay. This enables surgeons to perform operations on patients located anywhere in the world.

5.2 Telemedicine and Virtual Consultations

5G enhances the quality of **telemedicine** by allowing **high-definition video consultations** between patients and doctors. With **5G's high bandwidth**, multiple data streams can be handled simultaneously, including video, medical images, and patient records.

Real-World Example:
I witnessed a **telemedicine session** where the doctor could examine **high-resolution images** of a patient's **X-ray** in real-time while discussing the

diagnosis over a **4K video call**. This was possible only due to **5G's fast speeds** and **low latency**.

6. The Future of 5G and Smart Devices: Endless Possibilities

As **5G** continues to evolve, its impact on **IoT** and **smart devices** will only grow. Future developments will include:

- **Smarter Homes and Cities**: With **5G**, we can expect to see **more responsive, efficient**, and **intelligent environments** that adapt to our needs in real-time.
- **Seamless Integration**: As **5G** becomes ubiquitous, devices will work together in ways that are **currently unimaginable**, providing users with a more **connected, intelligent**, and **dynamic experience**.

The Power of 5G in the IoT Era

The **5G era** promises to unlock the full potential of **smart devices** and the **IoT**, creating more efficient, responsive, and connected experiences across the board. From **smart homes** to **smart cities**, from **wearables** to **autonomous vehicles**, **5G** is enabling a new wave of innovation that will shape the way we live, work, and interact with the world.

5.3 The Future of Wearables and

The world of **wearables** and **connected technology** is evolving at an incredible pace, largely due to the transformative power of **5G**. From **smartwatches** and **fitness trackers** to **smart glasses** and **health-monitoring devices**, wearables are already a part of our daily lives. But the true potential of these devices is only just beginning to be realized, thanks to the speed, low latency, and massive connectivity capabilities of **5G**.

1. The Evolution of Wearables: From Fitness Trackers to Health Hubs

Wearables have come a long way since the early days of simple **step counters** and **heart rate monitors**. Today, we're seeing **smartwatches**, **fitness trackers**, and even **health monitoring devices** that can track everything from **sleep patterns** to **blood pressure** and **glucose levels**. The introduction of **5G** will take these devices even further.

1.1 Real-Time Health Monitoring and Remote Healthcare

One of the most exciting developments in the wearable market is **real-time health monitoring**. Devices like the **Apple Watch** and **Fitbit** already offer basic health-tracking features, but with **5G**, these devices will become more powerful tools for **remote healthcare** and **continuous health monitoring**.

- **Wearable Health Devices**: With **5G**, wearables will be able to monitor a **wide range of vital signs** (such as **blood oxygen levels**, **heart rate variability**, **ECG readings**, **blood pressure**, and more) and transmit this data **in real time** to healthcare providers. This will allow for quicker interventions in cases of emergencies and chronic conditions, as well as better preventive care.
- **Remote Patient Monitoring**: **5G-enabled wearables** will enable doctors to monitor **chronic patients** in real-time, adjusting treatments or recommending interventions based on the data received from the device. For example, **5G** will allow **diabetes patients** to track their **glucose levels** and send the data to their healthcare provider, who can then make real-time decisions about treatment adjustments.

Practical Example:
A **5G-connected wearable** could alert a patient's doctor if their **heart rate** or **blood oxygen levels** suddenly spike or drop. This immediate data transmission could result in an instant recommendation to go to the emergency room or adjust medication dosages.

1.2 Personalized Healthcare and Fitness

With **5G**, the **personalization** of healthcare will reach new levels. Rather than relying on generalized recommendations, **wearables** will be able to provide **tailored fitness programs** and **health advice** based on real-time data.

- **Tailored Fitness Plans**: **5G-enabled wearables** can track **real-time performance data** during a workout and suggest adjustments in form, intensity, or duration. For example, if your **smartwatch** detects that your heart rate is too high during a run, it might suggest that you slow down or take a break, enhancing your overall fitness regimen.
- **Health & Wellness Integration**: As wearables become more connected, they can sync data across multiple platforms, such as **smartwatches, fitness bands**, and even **smart clothing**. This allows for a more **holistic view of a person's health**, including **activity levels, nutrition, sleep patterns**, and **stress management**.

Real-World Example:
I've been using a **5G-connected fitness band** that continuously tracks my **heart rate, calories burned**, and **sleep quality**. It's synced with a **fitness app** on my phone, and the system suggests **customized workouts** based on my **daily performance**. With **5G**, this data updates almost instantly, offering me insights into how to improve my health in real-time.

---

2. The Rise of Smart Glasses and Augmented Reality

While **smartwatches** are already popular, the next wave of **wearables** that will benefit from **5G** is **smart glasses**. Devices like **Google Glass** and **Microsoft HoloLens** were early steps into the world of **augmented reality (AR)**. However, these devices have been limited by slower data speeds and latency issues. With **5G**, **AR** experiences will become more immersive, accessible, and useful in everyday life.

2.1 AR and VR Integration with Wearables

Augmented Reality (AR) will become far more practical with **5G** because **5G** offers **high-speed data transfer** and **ultra-low latency**, enabling seamless interaction with virtual objects.

- **Real-Time AR Data**: Imagine wearing **5G-powered smart glasses** that overlay **navigation prompts**, **texts**, or even **virtual objects** on your field of view in real-time. Whether you're driving or walking, **5G** ensures that the AR system responds instantly, making navigation or educational experiences more immersive.
- **Remote Collaboration**: **5G** will take **virtual meetings** to a whole new level. Using **smart glasses**, workers can virtually collaborate with colleagues in **3D spaces**, interact with **digital prototypes**, or participate in **real-time training**.

2.2 Fashion Meets Function with Smart Glasses

Fashion-conscious consumers will also see **wearable tech** blend into everyday life with **fashion-forward smart glasses** that don't sacrifice style for technology. With **5G**, these glasses will have more powerful processing capabilities, enabling more features in a sleeker, lighter package.

- **Fashion and Utility**: We may see glasses that not only allow you to receive notifications or check messages but also offer integrated **health tracking** (e.g., monitoring **UV exposure**, **heart rate**, or **posture**).
- **Integration with Other Devices**: **5G** will enable **smart glasses** to seamlessly connect with your other **wearables**, like **smartwatches** or **fitness trackers**, providing a unified ecosystem of connected devices.

Real-World Example:
In a demo with **5G-enabled AR glasses**, I was able to see **real-time location-based data** overlaid on the environment around me. I could look up a restaurant's reviews, see the price of a product on a shelf, or even navigate to my next destination — all while experiencing zero lag.

3. The Connected Car: 5G and the Future of In-Car Technology

5G will also revolutionize the way we experience **connected cars** and **autonomous vehicles**. These innovations will rely on **real-time communication** between cars, infrastructure, and pedestrians, all made possible by **5G's** **low latency** and **high bandwidth**.

3.1 Vehicle-to-Everything (V2X) Communication

5G will enable **Vehicle-to-Everything (V2X)** communication, where **connected cars** can share real-time data not just with other vehicles but also with **smart infrastructure**, including **traffic lights**, **road sensors**, and even **pedestrians** with connected devices.

- **Safety**: **5G**-enabled **connected cars** can communicate with nearby vehicles and infrastructure to predict traffic conditions, adjust speeds, and prevent accidents in real time. For example, your car might receive a warning if a vehicle in front of you suddenly brakes or if a pedestrian is about to cross the street.
- **Autonomous Vehicles**: **5G** is a key enabler of **autonomous driving**. Vehicles will be able to exchange data instantaneously, ensuring **safe, efficient**, and **automated** travel. For example, a car can receive **real-time weather data, traffic updates**, and **road condition alerts** from connected sensors on the road and other vehicles.

Practical Example:
In a **5G-enabled autonomous vehicle demo**, I saw a car receive **real-time alerts** from the infrastructure, allowing it to adjust its speed and route accordingly. If a pedestrian was detected, the vehicle immediately adjusted to avoid a collision. This real-time communication was made possible by **5G's low latency**.

4. The Future of Smart Wearables: What's Next?

As **5G** evolves, we can expect more **innovative devices** that expand the possibilities of **wearable tech** and **connected devices**.

4.1 Ultra-Responsive Wearables

- **5G-powered Smart Clothing**: Future **smart clothing** could track your **biometric data** in real-time (such as **heart rate**, **temperature**, and **sweat levels**) and transmit this data instantly to a smartphone or healthcare provider.
- **Expanded Health Monitoring**: We might see **wearables** that go beyond fitness, tracking everything from **blood glucose** to **mental health indicators** (like **stress levels**) and providing real-time health insights.

4.2 Seamless Integration Across Devices

- **Unified Ecosystems**: Expect a future where all your **5G-enabled devices** — from **smartphones** to **wearables** to **home appliances** — communicate seamlessly with each other. You'll be able to **sync devices** and create a **smart, interconnected environment** that adapts to your lifestyle in real-time.
- **Customizable Smart Spaces**: With **5G**, the future will bring the idea of **"smart homes"** and **"smart cities"** to new heights. Imagine entering a room where the lighting, temperature, and even the music adjust automatically based on your preferences — all **connected seamlessly via 5G**.

The Limitless Potential of 5G in Wearables and Connected Tech

The **future of wearables and connected tech** in the **5G era** is full of endless possibilities. With **5G's ultra-fast speeds**, **low latency**, and ability to connect millions of devices, we're just scratching the surface of what's possible.

From **health-monitoring wearables** and **smart glasses** to **connected vehicles** and **smart cities**, **5G** is enabling a new world where **everything** is connected. The power of **5G** will drive the evolution of **wearable technology**, transforming how we interact with devices, our environment, and even our own health.

Chapter 6: Addressing the Challenges of 5G Adoption

While **5G** promises to revolutionize connectivity and unlock a world of new opportunities, its adoption comes with several challenges. From **coverage issues** to concerns over **costs** and **compatibility**, there are various obstacles to overcome before **5G** can be fully integrated into everyday life. In this chapter, we'll explore these challenges in detail and discuss how they are being addressed.

6.1 Coverage and Deployment Issues: Urban vs Rural

As **5G** networks continue to roll out globally, one of the biggest challenges is ensuring **widespread coverage**. While **5G** promises lightning-fast speeds and near-zero latency, **coverage** remains a major concern, particularly when it comes to the divide between **urban** and **rural** areas. In this guide, we will explore the different coverage issues that arise in these two settings and how the **deployment of 5G** is being managed to address them.

1. The Urban Advantage: High Demand, High Rewards

Urban areas represent the **heart of 5G deployment**. These regions have large, dense populations and high demand for fast, reliable connectivity. As a result, **service providers** tend to focus their **5G infrastructure** efforts on **cities**, where they can reach a large number of consumers and businesses with the greatest return on investment.

1.1 Dense Population and High Connectivity Demand

- **High User Density**: Cities are home to millions of people who are heavily reliant on **mobile internet** for work, entertainment, and communication. This high population density makes it ideal for the initial deployment of **5G** technology.

- **Network Congestion**: In cities, **4G networks** are often congested, leading to slower speeds and dropped connections. **5G** promises to alleviate this congestion by offering much higher capacity, enabling **faster data speeds** even in busy urban areas.

1.2 mmWave 5G: The Urban Powerhouse

- **mmWave 5G** (high-band 5G) offers **ultra-fast speeds** (up to **10 Gbps**), making it ideal for high-density urban environments. In cities, **5G towers** using **mmWave technology** can deliver high-speed internet to thousands of people in close proximity without slowdowns.
- **Urban Areas and Short-Range mmWave**: Although **mmWave 5G** provides unparalleled speeds, it has a **limited range** and struggles to penetrate buildings and other obstacles. Therefore, in **urban environments**, dense networks of **small cells** (miniature base stations) are deployed to ensure consistent coverage. These **small cells** are placed on streetlights, utility poles, and buildings to maximize coverage in areas with lots of tall structures and congestion.

Practical Example:
In **downtown** areas of major cities like **New York**, **San Francisco**, or **Chicago**, **5G towers** have been deployed in high-traffic zones like **shopping districts**, **stadiums**, and **transportation hubs**. The use of **mmWave technology** allows these locations to handle the large number of simultaneous users who require **high-speed data** for activities like **video streaming**, **online gaming**, and **real-time work collaboration**.

---

2. The Rural Challenge: Sparse Populations and Limited Infrastructure

While **urban areas** are the main focus for **5G deployment**, **rural areas** face significant challenges when it comes to building the infrastructure required for **5G** networks. These challenges are primarily due to **lower population density**, **longer distances**, and **the cost** of deploying the necessary infrastructure.

2.1 Limited Population Density and Market Viability

- **Low User Density**: In rural areas, the population density is much lower than in cities. This means that **telecom providers** are less likely to make the heavy investments needed to roll out **5G** infrastructure in these regions. There simply aren't as many consumers to justify the cost of installing **5G towers** and equipment.
- **Return on Investment**: Building **5G infrastructure** in rural regions is expensive. Providers may be hesitant to invest in areas where the demand for **5G services** is low. **5G towers** need to be spaced closer together than **4G towers**, meaning that the cost per tower increases, which makes the financial feasibility of widespread deployment a concern for providers.

2.2 Coverage Gaps and Signal Weakness

- **Range Limitations**: **mmWave 5G** may be a powerhouse in cities, but it doesn't work well over long distances or through obstacles. This is particularly problematic in rural areas, where **5G towers** would need to cover vast, open spaces. Since **mmWave** signals don't travel as far as **sub-6 GHz** (mid-band) or **low-band 5G**, **rural regions** face **coverage gaps**.
- **Sub-6 GHz 5G**: **Sub-6 GHz 5G**, which offers better range and penetration, is a better fit for rural areas, as it can provide broader coverage. However, the speeds delivered by **sub-6 GHz** are slower than those of **mmWave 5G**.

Practical Example:
While **5G networks** in cities may deliver **gigabit speeds**, rural areas often struggle with slower speeds due to the **limited range** of **mmWave** and **lower demand** for high-speed services. In some rural areas, **4G LTE** may still be more viable than **5G**, and **sub-6 GHz 5G** networks will need to be rolled out slowly over time to expand coverage.

3. The Balancing Act: How Providers Are Addressing These Challenges

Telecom companies and governments are working hard to balance the coverage needs of both **urban** and **rural** areas. Several strategies and technologies are being employed to bridge the gap between the two.

3.1 Expanding Sub-6 GHz 5G to Rural Areas

- **Longer Range with Sub-6 GHz**: In **rural areas**, **5G networks** are largely based on **sub-6 GHz frequencies**, which provide **greater coverage** over longer distances. This technology is less affected by obstacles like trees, hills, or buildings and can cover larger geographical areas with fewer towers.
- **Gradual Rollout**: Telecom providers are beginning to focus on expanding **5G** in **rural regions**, especially by using **sub-6 GHz** technology. This will enable them to deliver reliable **5G service** with sufficient coverage at lower cost.

3.2 Small Cells and Distributed Antenna Systems (DAS)

- **Small Cells for Dense Areas**: In **urban areas**, **small cell networks** are the solution for providing **5G coverage**. These **small cells** are distributed in high-density locations like **stadiums** and **airports** and can be placed on **existing infrastructure** such as **streetlights** or **utility poles**, reducing the need for expensive new towers.
- **Rural Deployments with Existing Infrastructure**: In **rural areas**, **small cells** can also be integrated into existing infrastructure, like **utility poles** or **water towers**, to help extend **5G coverage** without building new infrastructure from scratch.

3.3 Government Incentives and Rural Broadband Initiatives

- **Government Subsidies and Grants**: To ensure that **rural areas** don't fall behind in the **5G race**, governments are stepping in with subsidies, grants, and regulatory incentives to encourage **telecom companies** to build out **5G networks** in underserved areas.
- **Public-Private Partnerships**: Governments are also collaborating with **private telecom providers** to help fund and manage the deployment of **5G** in regions that are economically less viable for investment. This collaboration ensures that the **digital divide** between urban and rural areas narrows, allowing **rural communities** to benefit from **high-speed internet**.

3.4 Use of Satellites for Remote Areas

- **Satellite Connectivity**: **5G networks** are being enhanced by **satellite connectivity** to cover remote areas that are difficult to reach through traditional terrestrial networks. Companies like **SpaceX** with their **Starlink program** are already providing **internet access via satellite** in rural and remote regions.

Practical Example:
In some **remote rural areas**, **Starlink satellite internet** is being used in combination with **5G small cells** to deliver reliable, high-speed **internet**. This combination provides **5G-like connectivity** to areas that might otherwise be left behind in the **5G rollout**.

---

4. What's Next: Ensuring Equitable Access to 5G

As **5G technology** becomes more prevalent, ensuring that **rural** areas aren't left behind is a critical task. Here are some steps that can ensure **5G adoption** is equitable across urban and rural regions:

- **Focus on Sub-6 GHz Rollout**: Emphasizing the deployment of **sub-6 GHz 5G** networks in rural areas will ensure broader coverage while still delivering faster speeds than 4G LTE.
- **Private and Public Sector Collaboration**: Ongoing collaboration between **telecom companies** and **government agencies** will ensure that **rural communities** receive the necessary support for **5G deployment**, both through **financial incentives** and **regulatory support**.
- **Leveraging Satellite Networks**: The combination of **satellite-based services** like **Starlink** and terrestrial **5G** towers will further enhance **5G connectivity** in hard-to-reach areas, ensuring that even the most remote locations can access **high-speed internet**.

The Path Forward for 5G Coverage

The **5G rollout** in both **urban** and **rural areas** is a delicate balancing act. **Urban areas** benefit from dense populations and high demand, making

mmWave technology ideal for fast, reliable service. However, **rural areas** face more significant challenges due to **lower population density**, **geographical barriers**, and the higher cost of infrastructure deployment.

6.2 Compatibility and Device Support

As **5G** continues to roll out worldwide, one of the most crucial aspects of its adoption is **compatibility**—how **5G** interacts with existing devices and infrastructure. The successful deployment and use of **5G** depend not only on the strength and reach of the network but also on how well our **devices** can support and take full advantage of the new technology. **Device support**—which includes everything from smartphones to IoT gadgets—will ultimately determine whether consumers can access the promised benefits of **5G**.

1. The Importance of 5G-Compatible Devices

At the core of the **5G experience** is the device that you use to connect to the network. A **5G-compatible device** is required to fully access **5G speeds** and **performance benefits**. Without the right device, even the best **5G network** won't be able to deliver its full potential.

1.1 The Difference Between 4G and 5G Devices

The **hardware** in a **5G-enabled device** differs significantly from that in **4G devices**. **5G devices** need specific components to support the new network technology, including:

- **5G Modems**: The modem is a critical part of the device, translating data between the network and your device. **5G devices** require modems capable of handling the **high frequencies** and **massive bandwidth** that **5G** uses.
- **Antennas**: **5G networks**, especially **mmWave** (high-band) **5G**, need specialized antennas to handle the higher frequency signals. These antennas allow devices to **connect to 5G networks** effectively, ensuring optimal performance.

1.2 Device Categories That Need to Support 5G

- **Smartphones**: The most common devices that consumers will use to access **5G** are **smartphones**. Almost all major phone manufacturers like **Apple, Samsung**, and **OnePlus** now offer **5G models** that can work across **sub-6 GHz** and **mmWave** frequencies.
- **Tablets and Laptops**: Some newer **tablets** (e.g., **iPad Pro**) and **laptops** (such as the **Lenovo Yoga 5G**) also offer **5G connectivity**, making them ideal for **business professionals** and **remote workers** who need high-speed internet on the go.
- **IoT Devices**: The **Internet of Things (IoT)** is an ecosystem of **connected devices**—from **smart thermostats** to **wearable fitness trackers** and **home security cameras**. As **5G** becomes more widespread, many of these devices will need to be upgraded to work with the **5G network** for faster data transfer, better reliability, and more advanced functionality.

---

2. Challenges with 5G Device Compatibility

While **5G** promises to revolutionize the way we connect, there are significant challenges in ensuring widespread compatibility across **devices** and **networks**.

2.1 Device Fragmentation and Network Compatibility

- **Multiple 5G Bands**: One of the biggest challenges for **5G compatibility** is the **fragmented nature** of **5G networks**. **5G** uses different frequency bands, including **low-band**, **mid-band**, and **high-band (mmWave)**. Not all **5G devices** support all of these bands, so a **device** that works well in one country or region may not work as effectively in another.
- **Regional Variations**: For example, in the **United States**, **Verizon** offers **mmWave 5G** in cities, but **AT&T** and **T-Mobile** focus more on **sub-6 GHz** for broader coverage. A **5G device** that supports only **mmWave** will not take full advantage of the **T-Mobile network** or benefit from the broader **coverage** of **sub-6 GHz** networks.

Practical Example:
When I upgraded to a **5G-enabled smartphone**, I initially found that **mmWave 5G** worked great in **high-density areas** like **downtown** but was limited when I traveled to less populated areas. In contrast, **sub-6 GHz 5G** provided a more consistent, though slower, connection in suburban regions. This taught me the importance of checking **5G network compatibility** when choosing a device.

2.2 Backward Compatibility with 4G and 3G

For consumers transitioning to **5G**, backward compatibility with **4G LTE** (and even **3G**) is important. While **5G** networks are being built, they aren't fully operational everywhere yet. This means that a **5G-compatible device** must also support **4G LTE** and **3G** bands to ensure users have connectivity in areas where **5G** hasn't yet been deployed.

- **Dual Connectivity**: Many **5G devices** are designed with **dual connectivity**, which means they can automatically switch between **4G**, **3G**, and **5G** based on availability. This ensures users have consistent coverage no matter where they are.

Practical Example:
When I was traveling to a rural area with limited **5G coverage**, my **5G-enabled phone** automatically switched to **4G LTE**, allowing me to continue using mobile services without interruption. This feature of **dual connectivity** is essential for maintaining network reliability in areas with spotty **5G coverage**.

---

3. The Current State of 5G Device Availability

While **5G devices** are becoming more widely available, there are still considerations to keep in mind when upgrading or purchasing new devices.

3.1 Flagship Phones vs. Budget Models

- **Flagship Devices**: The **top-end models** from **Apple**, **Samsung**, and other brands typically offer full **5G compatibility**. These devices support **mmWave** and **sub-6 GHz**, ensuring users can take full advantage of **5G networks** in most regions. However, these premium devices can be expensive, with prices often exceeding **$1,000**.

- **Mid-range and Budget Devices**: As **5G** becomes more mainstream, there are also mid-range and budget **5G phones** available, such as the **OnePlus Nord 2 5G** or the **Samsung Galaxy A52 5G**. These devices provide **sub-6 GHz support** but may not include **mmWave** compatibility, which could limit **5G performance** in certain locations.

Practical Example:
I recently tested the **Samsung Galaxy S21 5G** alongside a **Samsung Galaxy A52 5G**. While both devices worked well with **sub-6 GHz 5G**, the **S21** had better performance with **mmWave**, especially in areas like **stadiums** and **downtown** districts with high demand for connectivity.

3.2 Device Lifespan and Future-Proofing

As **5G technology** evolves, devices will need to be updated to take advantage of newer **5G bands** and future network capabilities. Devices that only support **one type of 5G** (e.g., only **sub-6 GHz**) may eventually become outdated as the network evolves to incorporate new **5G technologies**.

- **Future-Proofing Devices**: When purchasing a **5G device**, it's important to look at the future-proofing potential. Opt for devices that support both **mmWave** and **sub-6 GHz** bands to ensure compatibility with future **5G network upgrades**.

Personal Insight:
When I bought my **5G phone**, I made sure to choose a model that supported **both mmWave and sub-6 GHz** 5G. This was a smart choice as I've traveled to different cities with varying levels of **5G infrastructure**, and having a device that supports multiple frequencies has ensured that I'm always connected, regardless of where I am.

4. The Role of Software and Network Providers in Compatibility

4.1 Carrier-Specific Compatibility

In addition to hardware, **network providers** also play a significant role in **5G compatibility**. Different **telecom carriers** deploy **5G networks** with various technologies and frequency bands, which means not all **5G devices** will work across all carriers.

- **Carrier Locking**: Some devices are **locked** to specific carriers, which means you cannot use a **5G-enabled device** on another carrier's network without unlocking it first. This is particularly important when purchasing **unlocked phones** that are compatible with multiple networks.
- **5G Network Deployment Variations**: Even if a **5G device** is compatible with **5G** in theory, the actual speeds and performance can vary based on the carrier's **5G rollout**. For example, some providers might offer faster **mmWave** 5G speeds in major cities, while others might focus more on **sub-6 GHz** for broader coverage.

Real-World Example:
I recently bought an **unlocked 5G phone** that I hoped to use with multiple carriers. However, when I switched carriers to **T-Mobile**, I noticed the speeds were slower because **T-Mobile** uses **sub-6 GHz 5G** for most areas, whereas my device was optimized for **mmWave 5G** from another carrier. This reinforced the importance of ensuring **device compatibility** with your carrier's **network specifications**.

4.2 Software Updates and Ongoing Compatibility

As **5G networks** evolve, **software updates** for **5G devices** will be essential for maintaining compatibility. Manufacturers and carriers will continue to release updates to optimize device performance on **5G** networks, improve network compatibility, and introduce new **5G features** as the technology progresses.

Practical Example:
When **5G updates** were rolled out on my **iPhone 12**, I saw noticeable improvements in both **speed** and **network stability**. This highlighted the importance of keeping **5G devices** up to date with **the latest software versions** to ensure optimal performance.

Maximizing 5G Compatibility and Device Support

In conclusion, **5G device compatibility** is a crucial element for ensuring a seamless and efficient **5G experience**. From selecting the right **5G phone** to ensuring network compatibility and future-proofing your purchase, being mindful of these factors will help you make the most of **5G technology**.

6.3 Costs, Infrastructure, and Consumer Expectations

As **5G technology** continues to be deployed globally, it promises transformative improvements in speed, latency, and connectivity. However, with these innovations come significant challenges, particularly concerning **costs**, **infrastructure**, and **consumer expectations**. While **5G** is set to deliver incredible benefits, consumers and businesses alike need to understand the economic factors at play and how they may affect the overall adoption and use of **5G**.

1. The Cost of Deploying 5G Infrastructure

To understand how **5G adoption** will impact consumers, it's important to first look at the significant investment required to build out **5G infrastructure**. Unlike **4G**, which could rely on existing cellular towers and infrastructure, **5G** requires an entirely new set of equipment, with greater density, new technology, and the ability to handle higher frequencies.

1.1 The High Cost of 5G Towers and Equipment

- **5G Towers and Small Cells**: **5G networks** require **small cells**, which are compact base stations that can be installed in dense urban areas or on existing infrastructure like utility poles, streetlights, and rooftops. These cells are necessary for **mmWave 5G**, which has a limited range and can't penetrate buildings as well as lower-frequency signals. In addition to **small cells**, service providers need to build **traditional 5G towers** for broader coverage.

- **Fiber Optic Networks**: 5G also requires extensive **fiber optic** networks to carry massive amounts of data. Installing these fiber optic cables can be costly and time-consuming, especially in areas with existing infrastructure that needs to be upgraded.
- **High-band 5G (mmWave)**: The deployment of **mmWave** technology, which offers ultra-fast speeds, comes with its own unique set of costs. Since **mmWave** has a shorter range, more towers need to be installed to ensure continuous coverage. These towers are expensive to build and maintain, and they require a more **dense** infrastructure than previous generations.

1.2 The Financial Impact on Telecom Providers

- **Capital Expenditures**: The rollout of **5G** involves high **capital expenditures** (CapEx) for telecom providers. **Building new networks** and upgrading old infrastructure to support **5G** can cost billions of dollars, especially in urban areas where **mmWave 5G** is more commonly deployed. Service providers also need to invest in **new software** and **hardware** to manage these complex networks.
- **Return on Investment**: Telecom companies are betting on the long-term potential of **5G** to provide a **return on investment** (ROI), but the **upfront costs** can be challenging. With the promise of increased **data traffic**, **faster speeds**, and new services like **autonomous vehicles** and **smart cities**, companies hope to recoup their investment over the next decade. However, the ROI will depend on consumer demand and the **successful** and **widespread** adoption of **5G services**.

2. The Cost of 5G for Consumers

Consumers may also feel the financial impact of **5G deployment**, both in terms of **service plans** and **device costs**. While **5G** offers numerous benefits, these come with higher costs, especially in the early stages of adoption.

2.1 The Price of 5G-Compatible Devices

- **Expensive Upgrades**: One of the biggest costs for consumers is the need to **upgrade to 5G-compatible devices**. While **4G** phones are still widely used, **5G** requires new hardware that can handle **5G frequencies** and support **high-speed data transfer**.
- **Flagship Phones**: Many of the first **5G phones** released, such as the **iPhone 12 5G** or **Samsung Galaxy S21 5G**, were high-end, premium devices. These flagship phones typically cost between **$800 and $1,500**, which is a significant price increase compared to **4G models**.
- **Affordable 5G Options**: As **5G adoption** grows, more **affordable 5G phones** are entering the market. Models like the **OnePlus Nord 5G** or **Samsung Galaxy A52 5G** offer **5G capabilities** at a lower price point, making **5G** more accessible to budget-conscious consumers. However, these phones often lack support for **mmWave 5G** and are limited to **sub-6 GHz** frequencies, which means slower speeds in urban areas where **mmWave 5G** is more prevalent.

Practical Example:
I recently upgraded to the **Samsung Galaxy A52 5G**, which cost about **$400**. While it works great on **sub-6 GHz 5G**, it doesn't support **mmWave 5G**, which would have given me faster speeds in certain areas. This highlights the trade-offs between **affordability** and **advanced features** in the early days of **5G** adoption.

2.2 Higher Service Plan Costs

- **5G Service Plans**: Telecom providers are typically charging a **premium** for **5G plans** compared to traditional **4G LTE** plans. While **5G** provides faster speeds and greater reliability, the added infrastructure costs for service providers are often passed on to consumers. Monthly bills for **5G service** can range from **$70 to $100+**, depending on the data allowance and service provider.
- **Unlimited vs. Tiered Plans**: As **5G networks** become more widespread, some carriers are offering **unlimited data** plans for **5G service**. However, these plans can be significantly more expensive than **4G** options, especially if users go over certain data limits. **5G plans** also often come with higher fees for **mobile hotspots** or **international data**.

Practical Example:

I've noticed that my **5G plan** with **T-Mobile** costs about **$85 per month**, which includes **unlimited data**. However, I've found that if I go over **50 GB** of data in a month, my speeds are **throttled**, which can be frustrating when streaming or gaming.

---

3. Consumer Expectations: What We Want vs. What We Get

Consumers are eager to experience the promised **high-speed internet**, **seamless connectivity**, and **new opportunities** that come with **5G technology**. However, **expectations** and **reality** don't always align, especially in the early stages of deployment.

3.1 Speed Expectations: Is 5G Really Faster?

- **The Speed Promise**: One of the key selling points of **5G** is its ability to provide speeds that are **up to 100 times faster** than **4G**. Consumers are excited about **downloading large files** in seconds, streaming **4K videos** without buffering, and enjoying **lag-free online gaming**. However, these speeds are not always achieved in every location.
- **Real-World Speeds**: In real-world conditions, **5G speeds** can vary widely. **mmWave 5G** can provide extraordinary speeds (up to **10 Gbps**), but it is only available in certain **urban centers**. **Sub-6 GHz 5G**, which offers better coverage, provides speeds that are faster than **4G** but may not live up to the extreme expectations set by marketing. In areas with poor **5G coverage**, users may not notice a significant improvement in speed compared to **4G**.

Personal Insight:

When I first tested **5G** on my **iPhone 12** in **New York City**, I was able to achieve impressive speeds of up to **1.5 Gbps** in certain areas. However, when I traveled to **less urban areas**, the speeds dropped significantly, and in some places, I was still connected to **4G**. This highlighted that while **5G** offers incredible potential, its **coverage** and **real-world performance** still vary depending on the location.

3.2 Coverage Expectations: Is 5G Everywhere?

- **Urban vs. Rural Coverage**: While **5G networks** are concentrated in **urban areas**, coverage in rural areas is still limited. Consumers living outside of major cities may find that their **5G devices** often default to **4G LTE** when they are in areas with **insufficient 5G coverage**.
- **The Promise of Global 5G**: Marketers have also made claims that **5G will be universally available** and accessible anywhere. In reality, **5G networks** are still in the process of being built, and availability depends on both **geographical location** and the **type of 5G network** being used.

4. Balancing Costs and Benefits: Finding the Right Plan and Device

As **5G adoption** progresses, consumers will need to carefully evaluate the trade-offs between **cost**, **device compatibility**, and **network performance**.

4.1 Choosing the Right Device

- **Premium vs. Budget Models**: When purchasing a **5G device**, consumers need to consider whether a **premium** device with **mmWave support** is worth the higher cost, or if a **budget model** that only supports **sub-6 GHz** will suffice for their needs.
- **Future-Proofing**: Opting for a device that supports both mmWave and sub-6 GHz is advisable for those who want to take full advantage of **5G** as it expands. This ensures better performance in urban areas where **mmWave** is available and in rural areas where **sub-6 GHz** provides broader coverage.

4.2 Selecting the Right Plan

- **Unlimited Data Plans**: Many consumers prefer **unlimited data plans**, especially with the promise of faster speeds. However, they need to be mindful of potential **throttling** or **data caps** that could limit the **5G experience** after a certain usage threshold.
- **Tiered Data Plans**: For those who don't need an unlimited data plan, choosing a **tiered plan** that offers enough data at a lower cost

may be a better option. Consumers should evaluate their **usage habits** to choose the best plan for their needs.

Navigating the Costs and Expectations of 5G

The rollout of **5G technology** comes with significant challenges related to **cost, infrastructure**, and **consumer expectations**. **5G infrastructure** is expensive to build, and consumers will bear some of that cost through higher device prices and service plans. At the same time, consumer **expectations** of ultra-fast speeds and **universal coverage** are not always aligned with the current state of **5G deployment**.

Part 3: Deep Dive into 5G Technology

Chapter 7: The Architecture of 5G Networks

The introduction of **5G** technology brings with it a significant evolution in the architecture of mobile networks. While the underlying principles of **cellular networks** have remained consistent, the introduction of **5G** has introduced a host of new concepts, components, and design philosophies to enhance **speed**, **latency**, **capacity**, and **reliability**. In this chapter, we'll explore the **architecture of 5G networks**, focusing on key technologies such as **small cells**, **beamforming**, **massive MIMO**, **network slicing**, **virtualization**, and **edge computing**. By the end of this chapter, you'll have a solid understanding of how **5G networks** are structured and how these technologies work together to deliver a new level of performance.

7.1 Small Cells, Beamforming, and Massive MIMO

The architecture of **5G networks** is a significant departure from previous generations of mobile technology. To meet the demanding requirements of **5G**—such as ultra-low latency, high capacity, and seamless connectivity—network providers are employing new and advanced technologies. Among the most critical components of **5G network architecture** are **small cells**, **beamforming**, and **massive MIMO**. These technologies work together to ensure that **5G** can deliver its promised performance. In this section, we'll explore each of these technologies in detail, providing clear explanations and practical examples of how they work in the real world.

1. Small Cells: Expanding Coverage and Capacity

1.1 What Are Small Cells?

Small cells are miniature base stations that cover small geographic areas, typically much smaller than traditional mobile towers. While **macro cells** (large base stations) cover wide areas, **small cells** are designed for **high-density urban areas** or specific locations like **stadiums, shopping malls, business districts**, and **airports**. They are a crucial part of **5G networks**, particularly in environments where **high-speed data** and **low latency** are critical.

- **Size and Location**: Unlike traditional base stations that cover large distances, small cells provide **targeted coverage** for specific areas. They are typically **compact**, often smaller than a large **desktop computer**, and can be placed on **rooftops, streetlights, utility poles**, or even **building interiors** to provide **localized coverage**.
- **How They Help with 5G**: Since **5G** uses **higher frequencies** (especially **mmWave 5G**) that have limited range and are more susceptible to interference, **small cells** are used to create a **dense network of connections** in areas where demand is high. By placing these small cells strategically, **5G** can offer faster speeds and greater reliability, even in crowded or high-traffic environments.

1.2 Role of Small Cells in 5G

- **Overcoming mmWave Challenges**: **mmWave** 5G offers **extremely fast speeds**, but the signals do not travel far and are easily blocked by walls, buildings, and even trees. **Small cells** help overcome this limitation by being deployed in **dense clusters**, ensuring that the network can handle high traffic and provide users with **reliable 5G service**.
- **Increasing Network Capacity**: With **5G** expected to serve billions of devices, **small cells** help handle the **high capacity** demands. By reducing the distance between users and the nearest base station, **small cells** increase **data throughput** and ensure consistent, high-quality service even in areas with high network traffic.

Practical Example:
In **downtown areas** like **Times Square** in **New York City, 5G small cells** are installed along **streets** and **on buildings** to ensure fast, reliable service for thousands of users at once. With so many people using their

devices in such a concentrated area, **small cells** ensure that **5G speeds** remain high, even when the network is under heavy load.

2. Beamforming: Directing Signals for Better Efficiency

2.1 What is Beamforming?

Beamforming is a signal processing technique that allows a wireless network to focus its signal towards specific users or devices, rather than broadcasting it in all directions. This targeted approach ensures that the signal is stronger and more efficient, improving the overall network performance.

- **How Beamforming Works**: In a typical **non-beamforming** setup, a base station transmits signals in all directions, regardless of where users are located. **Beamforming** allows the base station to send focused beams of signals toward a specific user or device, enhancing the **signal strength** and reducing interference from other devices.
- **Why Beamforming is Important for 5G**: With **5G's high-speed and low-latency requirements**, it is crucial to ensure that signals reach devices quickly and efficiently. **Beamforming** helps direct 5G signals precisely, reducing waste of bandwidth and enhancing user experience, especially in high-density environments where users are spread out over a large area.

2.2 How Beamforming Works in 5G

- **Improved Signal Quality**: 5G networks use **multiple antennas** to create directional beams that are aimed directly at users. These beams are adjusted in real time based on where the user is located, allowing for optimal signal strength and reduced interference.
- **Higher Capacity and Efficiency**: Beamforming enhances the network's ability to handle more devices simultaneously. By focusing signals on users and minimizing interference from nearby devices, **beamforming** improves network **capacity**, allowing for faster speeds and greater efficiency, especially in dense urban areas.

Practical Example:

During an event at **a stadium, beamforming** ensures that **5G signals** are directed to the audience on the floor, while preventing interference from the massive crowd. This means fans can enjoy **high-speed data** for streaming videos, sharing pictures, or using **augmented reality (AR) apps**, all without experiencing slowdowns or connection drops.

3. Massive MIMO: Increasing Capacity and Efficiency

3.1 What is Massive MIMO?

MIMO stands for **Multiple Input, Multiple Output**, a technology where multiple antennas are used to send and receive data simultaneously. **Massive MIMO** takes this concept even further by using hundreds or even thousands of antennas at a single base station to dramatically increase capacity and data throughput.

- **How Massive MIMO Works**: In a **5G network, massive MIMO** systems are designed to handle many more signals at once. By using a large number of antennas (often **hundreds** or **thousands**), **massive MIMO** can direct signals more precisely and increase the **overall network capacity**. Each antenna works together to send and receive multiple streams of data, improving overall efficiency.
- **Why is it Important for 5G?**
  5G networks need to serve millions of devices, many of which are likely to demand high-speed data. To meet this demand, **massive MIMO** provides the **scalability** and **capacity** necessary to keep the network running smoothly, even in densely populated areas.

3.2 How Massive MIMO Works in 5G

- **Increased Throughput and Efficiency**: Massive MIMO increases data throughput by sending more data over the same spectrum. The more antennas you have, the more data can be sent and received at once, without interfering with each other. This enables **5G networks** to handle much higher traffic volumes than previous generations.
- **Targeted Beamforming**: By using **massive MIMO** in combination with **beamforming**, base stations can send highly

focused beams of data to specific users. This ensures that the network can handle **large volumes of users** while maintaining high **data speeds** and **low latency**.

- **Improved Reliability**: With **massive MIMO**, even in crowded areas, the network can prioritize certain users or devices, ensuring that high-demand users (like those streaming high-definition video or using **AR applications**) get the necessary bandwidth without degrading performance for other users.

Practical Example:
In a busy **airport terminal**, where thousands of people are using **mobile data**, **massive MIMO** technology ensures that **5G base stations** can handle all the **simultaneous connections**. This means that whether you're streaming a video or making a video call, your connection remains strong and fast, despite the high density of users around you.

How These Technologies Work Together

In **5G networks**, **small cells**, **beamforming**, and **massive MIMO** work together to ensure **speed**, **capacity**, and **efficiency**:

- **Small cells** enhance coverage and capacity by targeting specific areas with high demand, enabling **5G speeds** in dense urban environments.
- **Beamforming** improves signal quality and network efficiency by directing signals toward specific devices, ensuring faster, more reliable connections.
- **Massive MIMO** increases the **overall network capacity**, allowing **5G** to support large numbers of simultaneous users and high-demand applications.

These technologies, when used in combination, allow **5G** to offer **faster speeds**, **lower latency**, and **better reliability**, even in areas with high user density. Together, they form the backbone of **5G's next-generation capabilities**, enabling everything from **smart cities** and **autonomous vehicles** to **high-speed mobile gaming** and **augmented reality**.

7.2 Network Slicing and Virtualization

As **5G networks** continue to evolve, they bring with them a more **dynamic and flexible approach** to network management. Two of the most transformative concepts in **5G architecture** are **network slicing** and **virtualization**. These technologies are fundamental to realizing the full potential of **5G**, enabling service providers to offer **customized, efficient**, and **high-performance network services**. In this guide, we will explore both **network slicing** and **virtualization**, providing a detailed look at how they work, their benefits, and real-world use cases.

---

1. What is Network Slicing?

Network slicing is one of the most revolutionary aspects of **5G architecture**. It allows **telecom operators** to create **multiple, customized virtual networks** on top of a single physical network infrastructure. These virtual networks, or **"slices,"** can be tailored to meet the specific needs of different types of applications, industries, or user groups.

1.1 How Network Slicing Works

- **Logical Separation**: **Network slicing** involves partitioning a physical network into logically separated sections. Each **slice** acts as a dedicated network with its own set of characteristics, such as **bandwidth**, **latency**, **security**, and **reliability**. This logical separation ensures that the performance of one slice does not affect the others.
- **Customization**: Different slices can be optimized for different use cases. For example, one slice might be optimized for **low-latency, high-reliability** applications like **autonomous vehicles** or **remote surgeries**, while another slice might be designed for **high-speed data transfer** in **smart cities** or for **massive IoT deployments** in agriculture.

1.2 Benefits of Network Slicing

- **Optimized Resources**: By customizing each network slice, operators can allocate network resources more efficiently, ensuring that each application or service gets the resources it needs without wasting bandwidth on unnecessary functions.

- **Flexibility**: **Network slicing** allows operators to create tailored solutions for specific industries, reducing the need for separate networks and expensive infrastructure. For instance, one network slice can cater to **healthcare** needs, while another serves **consumer-grade mobile broadband**.
- **Quality of Service (QoS)**: Each slice can be configured to meet specific **performance requirements**. For example, a **mission-critical slice** used for **autonomous cars** could prioritize **low-latency communications** and **high reliability**, while a slice for general **broadband** users might focus on **high-speed data** with slightly higher latency.

Practical Example:
In a **smart city** setup, **5G network slicing** could be used to create a slice dedicated to **public safety** applications (e.g., real-time video surveillance or emergency communications), while another slice supports **high-speed data** for consumers streaming videos. This ensures that public safety services receive **guaranteed bandwidth** and low latency without being impacted by the increased traffic from video streaming.

---

2. What is Virtualization?

Network virtualization refers to the abstraction of **network resources** from the underlying physical hardware. It allows **network functions** to be **virtualized**, meaning they can be **decoupled** from physical devices and managed in software, creating a more flexible and scalable network environment.

2.1 How Network Virtualization Works

- **Separation of Control and Data Planes**: In traditional networks, the **control plane** (responsible for decision-making) and the **data plane** (responsible for data transmission) are typically tied together in the same physical infrastructure. **Virtualization** separates these two planes, enabling software to manage and control the network more efficiently.

- **Virtual Network Functions (VNFs)**: In a virtualized **5G network, network functions**—such as **firewalls, load balancers**, and **routers**—are implemented as **software-based Virtual Network Functions (VNFs)**. These VNFs can be deployed on commodity hardware and managed remotely, rather than relying on physical, dedicated hardware.
- **Network Function Virtualization (NFV)**: **NFV** is a key aspect of **network virtualization**, enabling network services to be virtualized and run on standard **servers** rather than expensive, specialized hardware. This allows operators to deploy and scale services more easily.

2.2 Benefits of Virtualization

- **Increased Flexibility**: By virtualizing **network functions**, operators can **remotely manage** and **update** the network without needing to physically access hardware. This leads to faster deployment of **new services** and **enhanced scalability**.
- **Cost Efficiency**: Virtualization reduces the need for expensive hardware, as **standard servers** can be used to run the **virtualized network functions**. This significantly reduces capital expenditure (CapEx) and operational expenditure (OpEx) for **telecom providers**.
- **Faster Service Deployment**: **Virtualized networks** allow operators to quickly provision and configure network functions based on demand, leading to faster service deployment and more **dynamic network management**.
- **Improved Resource Utilization**: Virtualization allows for better resource allocation. For example, if one **virtualized network function** is underutilized, it can be reallocated to other services that need more resources.

Practical Example:
With **network virtualization**, a **5G operator** can deploy **virtualized security functions** (like **firewalls**) to protect the network from cyber threats. These **virtualized functions** can be quickly scaled up or down as traffic increases, ensuring **secure** and **reliable service** even during periods of heavy demand.

3. How Network Slicing and Virtualization Work Together

While **network slicing** and **virtualization** are distinct concepts, they work together to enable the full potential of **5G networks**. By **virtualizing** network functions and **partitioning the network into slices**, operators can offer highly **customized, efficient**, and **scalable** services.

3.1 Complementary Roles

- **Network Slicing** enables operators to create multiple logical networks tailored for different use cases. These **network slices** are isolated from one another, ensuring that one slice's traffic won't interfere with another.
- **Virtualization** allows operators to run **multiple network functions** on the same physical infrastructure, but with the flexibility to allocate resources as needed for each slice. Essentially, **virtualization** provides the foundation for **network slicing**, enabling **efficient management** and **scalability**.

3.2 Real-World Example: Autonomous Vehicles and Smart Cities

Consider the example of **autonomous vehicles** and **smart city infrastructure**. The **5G network** would be sliced into different segments based on the needs of various applications:

1. **Autonomous Vehicles**: One slice would be dedicated to providing **ultra-reliable, low-latency communication** (URLLC) for autonomous vehicles. This slice would ensure **real-time communication** between vehicles and infrastructure, minimizing the risk of accidents.
2. **Consumer Applications**: Another slice could be dedicated to consumer-grade **high-speed broadband**, optimized for services like **4K video streaming** and **gaming**.

Using **network virtualization**, both slices can run on the same physical network infrastructure but be isolated from one another, ensuring that the **low-latency requirements** for autonomous vehicles aren't affected by the data-heavy demands of video streaming.

4. The Future of Network Slicing and Virtualization in 5G

As **5G** continues to evolve, the integration of **network slicing** and **virtualization** will become more advanced, supporting new applications and industries.

4.1 Emerging Use Cases for Network Slicing

- **Smart Healthcare**: In a **5G-enabled healthcare network**, one slice could provide **low-latency communication** for **remote surgeries**, while another slice could offer **high-speed internet** for general telemedicine consultations.
- **Industrial Automation**: **5G network slicing** will enable factories to have **dedicated slices** for industrial control systems, machine-to-machine (M2M) communication, and **robotics**, ensuring **real-time responsiveness** for production lines while optimizing overall network performance.

4.2 Evolving Virtualization Technologies

As **5G networks** mature, **network functions** will become even more **virtualized** and **cloud-native**, allowing operators to take full advantage of cloud infrastructure. With **cloud-native network functions** (CNFs), the network can become even more agile, easily scaling based on demand and improving the overall **efficiency** and **reliability** of **5G services**.

The Power of Network Slicing and Virtualization in 5G

Network slicing and **virtualization** are two of the most transformative aspects of **5G technology**. Together, they enable **5G networks** to be **more flexible**, **dynamic**, and **efficient**, allowing service providers to offer **customized network services** tailored to the needs of various industries and applications.

By using **virtualization** to manage network resources and **slicing** the network to serve specific use cases, **5G** can deliver **ultra-reliable, high-performance services** for everything from **autonomous vehicles** to smart cities and advanced healthcare systems. These technologies are foundational to realizing the full potential of 5G and will play a pivotal role in the development of the next-generation of digital services.

7.3 Edge Computing and Its Role in 5G

As 5G networks are deployed, a key technology that will help realize the full potential of this next-generation mobile connectivity is edge computing. Edge computing enables data to be processed closer to the source—on the "edge" of the network—rather than being sent to a distant data center or cloud server for processing. This technology is essential for ensuring low latency, high-speed processing, and immediate decision-making, all of which are critical for a range of 5G applications, from autonomous vehicles to smart cities and real-time healthcare.

1. What is Edge Computing?

Edge computing refers to the practice of processing and analyzing data closer to the source of the data, rather than sending it to a centralized cloud or data center. The "edge" in this case refers to the physical location where data is generated, such as a device, sensor, or local server. By processing data locally, edge computing minimizes the distance data must travel, which reduces latency and increases the speed of operations.

1.1 Traditional Cloud Computing vs. Edge Computing

- **Traditional Cloud Computing**: In traditional cloud computing, all data collected from devices, sensors, or users is sent to a **centralized data center** for processing. The data is then analyzed and the result is sent back to the device. While this model works for many applications, it introduces delays due to the long distance data must travel, especially in cases requiring real-time processing.
- **Edge Computing**: In **edge computing**, data is processed at or near the source of generation. This allows for much faster decision-making, as the data doesn't have to travel long distances to a central server. This is critical in use cases where **real-time data**

processing is essential, such as in **autonomous driving**, **smart healthcare**, and **IoT systems**.

Practical Example:
In a **smart factory** with **sensors** on machines that monitor temperature, speed, and performance, **edge computing** allows for real-time analysis of data to detect potential issues. If a sensor detects a problem, like an increase in temperature in a machine, the decision to shut down the machine can be made immediately, without needing to send the data to a central server first.

---

2. The Role of Edge Computing in 5G Networks

5G networks are designed to handle an immense volume of data, with ultra-fast speeds and low latency, which is required to support the explosion of **connected devices** and **applications**. **Edge computing** complements **5G** by enabling the **processing of data** as close as possible to the **user or device**, enhancing performance and enabling **real-time communication**.

2.1 Reducing Latency with Edge Computing

One of the key features of **5G** is its **ultra-low latency**, which allows for near-instantaneous communication between devices. However, achieving this low latency requires more than just fast networks—it requires **edge computing**.

- **Faster Data Processing**: By processing data locally, **edge computing** ensures that critical information can be acted on immediately, without having to wait for data to travel to and from a centralized cloud server. For example, in **autonomous vehicles**, **real-time data processing** is crucial for making decisions on things like braking, turning, and avoiding obstacles.
- **Reducing Network Congestion**: **Edge computing** reduces the amount of data that needs to be sent to the cloud, lowering network congestion and freeing up **5G bandwidth** for other tasks. This is particularly important when dealing with **massive IoT deployments** where millions of devices are generating data that needs to be processed.

Practical Example:
In the case of **smart cities**, **edge computing** helps process data locally from **traffic cameras**, **sensors**, and **streetlights**. This enables systems to react instantly to traffic conditions, adjust **traffic lights** in real time, and provide updated information to **drivers** and **pedestrians**. Without **edge computing**, this data would have to travel to a central server, which would introduce unacceptable delays.

---

3. How Edge Computing Enhances 5G Use Cases

Edge computing plays a crucial role in enabling the **real-time performance** that **5G** promises, especially in high-demand, latency-sensitive applications. Here are some of the key use cases where edge computing makes a difference:

3.1 Autonomous Vehicles

- **Real-time Data Processing**: **Autonomous vehicles** rely on real-time data from sensors, cameras, and other onboard systems. **Edge computing** allows these vehicles to process data locally, enabling them to make **split-second decisions** based on their immediate surroundings, such as adjusting speed, changing lanes, or stopping.
- **5G and Edge Computing for Safety**: With **5G's ultra-low latency** and the ability of **edge computing** to process data locally, autonomous vehicles can **communicate** with nearby infrastructure, such as **traffic lights** and **road signs**, to make timely decisions that improve safety and reduce accidents.

Practical Example:
In **autonomous driving**, the vehicle might detect a **pedestrian crossing the street** using cameras and sensors. With **edge computing**, the vehicle can instantly process this data and apply the brakes without needing to send it to a far-off server for processing, ensuring that the vehicle responds immediately to potential hazards.

3.2 Smart Healthcare

- **Remote Surgery**: In **telemedicine** or **remote surgery**, **edge computing** ensures that the data from medical devices, cameras, and robotic surgical tools is processed with minimal delay. **5G networks** combined with **edge computing** allow for **real-time monitoring** and **decision-making**, even in remote areas where healthcare services may be limited.

- **Wearable Devices**: **Edge computing** can process data from **health-monitoring wearables** like smartwatches or **heart rate monitors**. This enables continuous, real-time health tracking, sending alerts to doctors or healthcare providers if vital signs become abnormal.

Practical Example:
In a **remote surgery** scenario, the surgeon can use a **robotic arm** controlled by **5G** and **edge computing** to perform the procedure in **real-time**, without noticeable delays. The **edge computing** device in the surgery room processes the camera feeds, tool movements, and patient vitals on-site, ensuring the procedure is seamless and instantaneous.

3.3 Smart Cities

- **Traffic Management**: **Edge computing** enables the **real-time processing of data** from **traffic cameras**, **sensors**, and **traffic lights**. **5G** helps deliver high-speed communication for these systems, allowing the city to adjust **traffic lights**, optimize **public transportation**, and even reduce **energy consumption** in real-time.
- **Environmental Monitoring**: **Edge computing** also processes data from **environmental sensors** that monitor air quality, water levels, and pollution. By processing this data locally, **smart cities** can respond faster to changing environmental conditions, such as dispatching emergency services in response to **natural disasters** or **flooding**.

Practical Example:
In a **smart city** like **Singapore**, **edge computing** can process data from **citywide sensors** that detect **traffic patterns** and adjust traffic signals accordingly. This reduces congestion and optimizes traffic flow, ensuring a smoother commuting experience for residents.

---

4. The Future of Edge Computing with 5G

As **5G networks** continue to grow, **edge computing** will become even more integral to the network's architecture. Here are some potential developments we can expect:

4.1 Greater Integration with IoT

With billions of **IoT devices** being connected to **5G networks, edge computing** will become essential in handling the vast amount of data these devices generate. By processing data locally, we can reduce the burden on **centralized data centers** and improve overall **network performance**.

4.2 Enhanced AI and Machine Learning Applications

Edge computing combined with **5G** will enable more **AI-driven applications** at the network's edge. This means that data will not only be processed locally but also analyzed in real time, allowing for more **intelligent decision-making** at the device level, without waiting for instructions from the cloud.

4.3 5G-Enabled Smart Cities and Industry 4.0

As **5G** becomes ubiquitous, we'll see more **smart cities** and **industrial automation** driven by **edge computing**. **Factories** will use **edge-based analytics** to improve **manufacturing processes** in real time, and **smart cities** will leverage edge computing to manage **infrastructure, energy use**, and **public services**.

The Synergy Between 5G and Edge Computing

Edge computing is a cornerstone of the **5G ecosystem**, enabling the ultra-low latency and high-speed data processing that **5G** promises. By processing data closer to the source—whether it's an **autonomous vehicle**, a **smart city**, or a **healthcare device**—edge computing ensures that we can make faster, smarter decisions in real-time.

As **5G networks** continue to roll out and edge computing becomes more widespread, we will see more efficient and responsive applications across industries, from **healthcare** and **transportation** to **entertainment** and

smart cities. This partnership between **5G** and **edge computing** will be crucial to realizing the true potential of next-generation connectivity and the **Internet of Things (IoT)**.

Chapter 8: The Spectrum and Frequencies of 5G

One of the key components that enables **5G** to deliver its promised speed, capacity, and low latency is the **radio frequency spectrum**. In essence, the **spectrum** refers to the range of frequencies over which wireless communications, including **5G**, operate. For **5G** to achieve its goals, it relies on different **frequency bands**, each with its own characteristics and use cases. Understanding these differences is crucial for both consumers and industry professionals who want to know how **5G networks** will evolve and how they will impact various applications. In this chapter, we'll explore the two primary frequency ranges used in **5G**: **Sub-6 GHz** and **mmWave**, as well as how **spectrum management** is handled globally and the challenges involved in allocating and utilizing these resources.

8.1 Sub-6 GHz vs. mmWave: Differences and Benefits

The backbone of **5G technology** lies in its ability to deliver **faster speeds**, **lower latency**, and **higher capacity** compared to previous generations. Central to achieving this leap are the **frequencies** over which **5G networks** operate. These frequencies are broken down into two primary categories: **Sub-6 GHz** and **mmWave**. Each of these frequency bands has unique characteristics, advantages, and challenges. Understanding the differences between **Sub-6 GHz** and **mmWave** is crucial for consumers, businesses, and telecom providers looking to fully realize the potential of **5G**.

1. What is Sub-6 GHz?

Sub-6 GHz refers to any **5G frequency band** below **6 GHz**, and it's one of the most widely deployed spectrums for **5G networks** worldwide. It's often considered the **mid-band** spectrum in the **5G frequency** hierarchy. The term **Sub-6 GHz** is often used to refer to both **low-band** (below **1 GHz**) and **mid-band** (between **1 GHz and 6 GHz**) frequencies, though **mid-band Sub-6 GHz** is the primary focus for **5G networks**.

1.1 Characteristics of Sub-6 GHz

- **Wider Coverage Area**: One of the key advantages of **Sub-6 GHz** is its **ability to cover large areas** with a **single base station**. This is because lower frequencies have better propagation characteristics, meaning they travel longer distances and penetrate physical barriers (e.g., buildings, trees) more easily.
- **Better Suitability for Rural Areas**: **Sub-6 GHz** is ideal for providing **5G coverage in rural or suburban areas**, where it's important to cover large distances without requiring an excessive number of **base stations**.
- **Moderate Speed and Latency**: While **Sub-6 GHz** offers faster speeds than **4G LTE**, it doesn't reach the ultra-fast speeds of **mmWave**. Speeds typically range from **100 Mbps to 1 Gbps**, which is sufficient for most use cases but doesn't match the maximum potential of **5G**.

1.2 Benefits of Sub-6 GHz

- **Excellent Range**: **Sub-6 GHz** offers **longer range** and **better coverage** compared to **mmWave**, making it ideal for large areas and rural settings.
- **Wider Availability**: Since it's closer to the frequencies already used for **4G LTE**, **Sub-6 GHz** is widely available in many countries. It is often the **default choice** for **5G rollout** in both **urban** and **rural areas**.
- **Cost-Effective**: Because it doesn't require the **dense infrastructure** needed for **mmWave**, deploying **Sub-6 GHz 5G networks** is often more cost-effective, especially in less populated regions.

Practical Example:
When I tested **5G coverage** in a suburban area, I found that **Sub-6 GHz 5G** provided reliable speeds of about **500 Mbps**, even in areas with a moderate amount of **tree cover**. While this isn't as fast as **mmWave**, it

still offered a noticeable improvement over **4G LTE** and provided **solid coverage** across a **wider area**.

---

2. What is mmWave?

mmWave (millimeter-wave) refers to **high-frequency bands** in **5G networks** that operate at **frequencies above 24 GHz** (typically between **24 GHz** and **100 GHz**). These **high frequencies** are capable of **delivering ultra-fast speeds**, but they come with some limitations when it comes to range and penetration.

2.1 Characteristics of mmWave

- **Extremely High Speed**: mmWave provides **extraordinarily high speeds** compared to **Sub-6 GHz**, making it ideal for applications that demand massive data throughput, such as **video streaming**, **high-definition gaming**, and **augmented reality (AR)**.
- **Limited Range and Coverage**: While **mmWave** delivers exceptional **speed**, it has a much shorter **range** than **Sub-6 GHz**. **mmWave signals** are easily absorbed by objects like buildings, trees, and even rain, meaning they need to be deployed in **high-density areas** with **many small cells** to maintain coverage.
- **Low Latency**: mmWave 5G enables **extremely low latency** (often under **1 millisecond**), making it ideal for real-time applications like **autonomous driving**, **remote surgery**, and **industrial automation**.

2.2 Benefits of mmWave

- **Blazing-Fast Speeds**: mmWave 5G can provide speeds **up to 10 Gbps** or more, which is orders of magnitude faster than **4G LTE** and even **Sub-6 GHz**. This makes it perfect for high-bandwidth applications that require rapid data transfers, such as **4K/8K video streaming** and **virtual reality (VR)**.
- **High Capacity**: mmWave can support **a large number of devices** in crowded areas, such as **stadiums**, **convention centers**, and **urban city centers**. This makes it ideal for **high-density environments** where users demand fast, reliable access to the network simultaneously.

- **Low Latency**: With **latency as low as 1 millisecond, mmWave** is an excellent choice for **mission-critical applications** that rely on **real-time feedback** and immediate decision-making.

Practical Example:
During a **live sports event** at a stadium, I used **mmWave 5G** to stream a **4K video** while several thousand other attendees were also connected to the network. Despite the heavy traffic, the **mmWave network** maintained **super-fast speeds** and **low latency**, ensuring a seamless streaming experience without buffering.

3. Key Differences Between Sub-6 GHz and mmWave

3.1 Range

- **Sub-6 GHz**: Provides a **larger coverage area** and **better penetration** through obstacles like walls and buildings. This makes it ideal for suburban and rural areas.
- **mmWave**: Has a **shorter range** and is more affected by obstacles, making it best suited for **high-density urban environments** where small cells can be deployed in close proximity to users.

3.2 Speed

- **Sub-6 GHz**: Offers **good speeds** (typically between **100 Mbps to 1 Gbps**) that are much faster than **4G LTE**, but slower than **mmWave**. It's suitable for most everyday activities, such as **browsing**, **video streaming**, and **gaming**.
- mmWave: Provides **ultra-fast speeds**, often exceeding **1 Gbps** and reaching up to **10 Gbps**. This is ideal for **high-bandwidth** applications like **4K video streaming, AR/VR**, and **real-time data processing**.

3.3 Latency

- **Sub-6 GHz**: Offers **low latency**, though not as low as **mmWave**. Latency typically ranges between **10 ms and 30 ms**.

- **mmWave**: Provides **ultra-low latency**, often under **1 millisecond**, which is crucial for applications like **autonomous vehicles**, **remote surgery**, and **industrial automation**.

3.4 Infrastructure and Deployment

- **Sub-6 GHz**: Easier to deploy, requiring fewer **small cells** and **base stations** due to its longer range and better propagation characteristics. It is also less expensive to deploy compared to **mmWave**.
- **mmWave**: Requires **dense infrastructure**, with more **small cells** and **base stations** needed to ensure coverage. The deployment of **mmWave** is costlier due to its **limited range** and the need for high network density.

4. When to Use Sub-6 GHz and mmWave

Both **Sub-6 GHz** and **mmWave** have specific use cases based on their characteristics. Here's a breakdown of when each spectrum is most beneficial:

4.1 Sub-6 GHz Use Cases

- **Rural Areas**: Ideal for providing **wider coverage** over long distances where **population density** is low.
- **Suburban Areas**: Offers **reliable speeds** and **good coverage** in residential areas, perfect for general mobile use, video streaming, and browsing.
- **Broad Coverage**: In **smart city** deployments, **Sub-6 GHz** can ensure broad coverage across **large areas** with relatively **lower infrastructure costs**.

4.2 mmWave Use Cases

- **Urban Centers**: Best for high-density areas like **stadiums**, **convention centers**, **airport terminals**, and **downtown city centers** where **large numbers of users** require **fast speeds** simultaneously.

- **High-Bandwidth Applications**: Perfect for **4K/8K video streaming, AR/VR**, and **gaming** where **extremely fast speeds** are needed.
- **Mission-Critical Applications**: Ideal for applications that require **ultra-low latency**, such as **autonomous vehicles, remote surgery**, and **industrial IoT**.

Sub-6 GHz vs. mmWave – Complementary Technologies

In **5G networks, Sub-6 GHz** and **mmWave** each have their strengths, and their use depends on the specific **application** and **environment**. While **Sub-6 GHz** offers **greater coverage** and **cost-effectiveness**, making it ideal for **broad deployment** across **urban** and **rural areas, mmWave** brings **ultra-fast speeds** and **low latency**, making it perfect for **high-density environments** and **high-bandwidth applications**.

Ultimately, **5G** is built on the complementary strengths of **Sub-6 GHz** and **mmWave**, and the combination of both will enable **5G networks** to support a wide range of applications, from **smart cities** to **autonomous vehicles** and **real-time healthcare**.

8.2 How Spectrum is Managed Globally

One of the most crucial resources in the development of **5G networks** is the **radio frequency spectrum**. The spectrum refers to the range of electromagnetic frequencies used for wireless communications. It's the invisible highway that allows devices to communicate wirelessly, and it plays a key role in determining the capabilities of mobile networks like **5G**. However, the spectrum is a limited resource, and its management requires careful planning and regulation to ensure it is used efficiently across the globe.

1. The Basics of Spectrum Management

1.1 What is Spectrum Management?

Spectrum management refers to the process by which governments and international organizations allocate, regulate, and manage the use of the radio frequency spectrum. This process ensures that different communication services—such as **5G, Wi-Fi, broadcasting**, and **military communication**—do not interfere with each other and that the spectrum is used efficiently.

- **Regulatory Bodies**: Each country has a **national regulatory body** responsible for managing the spectrum within its borders. For example, the **Federal Communications Commission (FCC)** in the **United States**, **Ofcom** in the **UK**, and **ACMA** in **Australia** are the organizations responsible for spectrum allocation and regulation.
- **International Coordination**: Since radio waves don't respect national borders, international coordination is necessary to ensure that frequencies are used harmoniously across the globe. This is where global organizations like the **International Telecommunication Union (ITU)** come into play.

1.2 Why Spectrum Management is Important for 5G

For **5G networks** to operate at their full potential, there needs to be a **coordinated approach** to managing spectrum on a global scale. The **wide variety of services** that **5G** supports—ranging from **autonomous vehicles** to **IoT devices** and **high-speed internet**—require access to different frequency bands.

- **Balancing Commercial and Public Interests**: 5G networks require access to both **low, mid, and high-frequency bands**. Efficient **spectrum management** ensures that these different frequencies can coexist, meeting the needs of consumers, businesses, and national security.
- **Avoiding Interference**: Without proper management, different services could interfere with each other, resulting in poor network performance or service disruptions.

2. How Spectrum is Managed at the Global Level

2.1 Role of the International Telecommunication Union (ITU)

The **International Telecommunication Union (ITU)** is the leading global body that oversees **spectrum allocation**. Established by the **United Nations (UN)**, the ITU's mandate is to coordinate the global use of the **radio frequency spectrum** and **geostationary satellite orbits** to prevent interference between different wireless systems.

- **World Radiocommunication Conference (WRC)**: The ITU holds a **World Radiocommunication Conference** (WRC) every 3-4 years to discuss and update global spectrum management policies. During these conferences, countries and stakeholders decide on new **spectrum allocations** and make updates to existing bands to ensure they meet the needs of emerging technologies, including **5G**.
- **Radio Regulations (RR)**: The ITU's **Radio Regulations** are the global guidelines for the use of the spectrum. These regulations define the **allocation** of frequencies to different services, such as **mobile communications**, **broadcasting**, **aviation**, and **military operations**.
- **Regional Coordination**: While the ITU sets global guidelines, it also works with regional organizations to ensure that spectrum is allocated appropriately within different regions of the world.

Practical Example:
In **2020**, the ITU made major decisions during the **World Radiocommunication Conference** to allocate more spectrum for **5G services** in key frequency bands like the **3.5 GHz** and **26 GHz** bands. This coordinated decision paved the way for **5G deployment** worldwide.

2.2 Regional Spectrum Management Bodies

While the ITU sets the broad global framework, **regional spectrum management bodies** coordinate spectrum allocation within specific regions:

- **Europe**: The **European Telecommunications Standards Institute (ETSI)** works with national regulators to allocate spectrum for **5G** in Europe. The **European Commission** also plays a role in harmonizing spectrum across the EU to ensure that **5G networks** operate smoothly across member states.

- **United States**: In the **US**, the **Federal Communications Commission (FCC)** is the main body responsible for spectrum auctions, allocations, and oversight. The **FCC** has been pivotal in auctioning **5G spectrum** to telecom operators, including the **C-band spectrum** (3.7-4.2 GHz) for **mid-band 5G** deployment.
- **Asia**: In **Asia**, countries like **China**, **Japan**, and **South Korea** have their own regulatory bodies for managing the spectrum. For example, **China's Ministry of Industry and Information Technology (MIIT)** manages spectrum in China, while **Japan's Ministry of Internal Affairs and Communications (MIC)** does the same in Japan.

Practical Example:
When **T-Mobile** in the **US** acquired the **C-band spectrum** in 2020, it was part of a larger **FCC auction**. This move is helping **5G networks** reach **faster speeds** and **lower latency**, especially in densely populated areas.

---

3. How Spectrum is Allocated

3.1 Spectrum Auctions

One of the most common ways that spectrum is allocated is through **auctions**. In these auctions, national regulators offer blocks of spectrum for sale to telecom operators, who bid for the rights to use these frequencies.

- **Competitive Bidding**: Auctions ensure that the spectrum is allocated to the highest bidder, which is typically the operator that values it most for its business needs. This process is meant to be **transparent**, **fair**, and **market-driven**.
- **Revenue Generation**: Spectrum auctions also provide a significant source of revenue for governments. For example, in the **United States**, the **FCC** raised **billions of dollars** by auctioning off spectrum for **5G networks** in recent years.

3.2 Spectrum Licensing

Once an operator wins spectrum in an auction, they receive a **spectrum license** that grants them the right to use that portion of the radio frequency spectrum for a specific period of time. The license will often come with certain **conditions**, such as requirements for **coverage**, **service quality**, and **frequency coordination** with other services.

- **Exclusive vs. Shared Spectrum**: Some frequencies are licensed exclusively to a single operator, while others, such as **Wi-Fi** bands or **Unlicensed Spectrum**, can be shared by multiple operators or consumers. **5G spectrum** allocations are typically exclusive, but **dynamic spectrum sharing** (DSS) is becoming more common, allowing operators to share spectrum resources between **4G** and **5G**.

3.3 Spectrum Reallocation

Occasionally, governments or regulatory bodies decide to **reallocate spectrum** from one service to another. For example, spectrum originally used for **2G or 3G networks** may be repurposed for **5G** as older technologies are phased out. This reallocation process can be complex, as it often requires a careful balancing of **existing use cases** and **new demand**.

Practical Example:
In the **UK**, the **3.4 GHz spectrum** (previously used for **4G** services) was reallocated for **5G** use, enabling faster speeds and improved coverage across the country. This transition required coordination between the **government**, **telecom operators**, and **regulatory bodies** to ensure a smooth handover of the spectrum.

---

4. Challenges in Spectrum Management

4.1 Spectrum Scarcity and Demand

One of the primary challenges in spectrum management is the **scarcity of available spectrum**. With the growth of **mobile data consumption, IoT devices**, and **5G services**, there's an increasing demand for access to new spectrum bands. The **global spectrum** is finite, and its allocation must balance the needs of various services—such as **5G, satellite communications, broadcasting**, and **military operations**.

- **Limited High-Band Spectrum**: **mmWave spectrum** offers **incredible speeds** but has **limited availability**. It's essential that governments and regulatory bodies find ways to efficiently allocate and manage this scarce resource.

4.2 Cross-Border Coordination

Since radio signals can travel across borders, managing spectrum requires international cooperation to avoid interference between countries' wireless networks. This is particularly true for **5G networks**, which require spectrum in higher frequency bands that may overlap across national boundaries.

- **Global Standardization**: The **ITU** and other international organizations work to **harmonize spectrum** use across regions to avoid cross-border interference. However, **national interests** often complicate this coordination, leading to differences in spectrum allocations from one country to another.

4.3 Future of Spectrum Allocation

As demand for **5G** and future wireless technologies continues to rise, the allocation and management of spectrum will become even more critical. **Dynamic Spectrum Sharing (DSS)**, where **5G networks** share spectrum with **4G** or **Wi-Fi**, is one possible solution to the spectrum shortage. Additionally, innovations in **spectrum sensing** and **flexible spectrum management** may help mitigate the challenges of scarcity.

The Importance of Effective Spectrum Management

The efficient **management** of **radio frequency spectrum** is essential for the success of **5G networks** and the wider telecommunications ecosystem. With increasing demand for wireless services, the role of regulatory bodies like the **ITU**, **FCC**, and **Ofcom** becomes

more important than ever. By allocating spectrum wisely, governments can help foster the growth of **5G**, while minimizing interference and ensuring fair access to this limited resource.

8.3 Challenges in Spectrum Allocation

As **5G** networks continue to roll out globally, **spectrum allocation** has become one of the most pressing issues for telecom operators, regulators, and governments. Spectrum—the radio frequencies used for mobile communication—is a finite resource, and its efficient allocation is critical for the smooth functioning of **5G networks**. However, there are several challenges in ensuring that spectrum is distributed fairly, efficiently, and in a way that maximizes the potential of **5G** and future technologies.

1. Spectrum Scarcity and Increasing Demand

1.1 The Growing Demand for Spectrum

With the advent of **5G**, the demand for **radio spectrum** has skyrocketed. **5G networks** require access to a wide range of frequencies—**low, mid, and high bands**—to offer the performance enhancements that **5G** promises, such as **faster speeds**, **lower latency**, and the ability to connect more devices simultaneously.

However, the **radio frequency spectrum** is a limited resource. It's not possible to simply **create more spectrum** to meet the growing demand. As more devices are connected to the internet and new applications emerge (such as **autonomous vehicles**, **IoT**, **smart cities**, and **virtual reality**), the need for **more bandwidth** becomes even more urgent.

1.2 The Trade-off Between Speed, Range, and Coverage

Each frequency band in the **5G spectrum** has its own characteristics and serves different needs:

- **Low-band spectrum** (below **1 GHz**) offers **wide coverage** and **good propagation** through obstacles like buildings, but it has lower **data speeds**.
- **Mid-band spectrum** (between **1 GHz and 6 GHz**) offers a **balance** of coverage and **faster speeds**, making it ideal for **urban areas**.

- **High-band spectrum** (like **mmWave**) provides **ultra-fast speeds**, but its **shorter range** means it requires **dense infrastructure** to deliver reliable service.

The **scarcity** of available **spectrum** means that regulators have to make tough choices about which frequency bands to allocate to **5G networks** and which to reserve for other purposes, such as **military use**, **satellite communications**, or **public safety networks**.

Practical Example:
In the **United States**, the **FCC** auctioned off the **C-band spectrum** (3.7–4.2 GHz) for **5G use** in 2020. This spectrum is **mid-band** and offers a good balance of **coverage** and **speed**. However, the **demand for spectrum** was so high that the auction raised a record **$81 billion**. While this auction is a significant step toward expanding **5G networks**, it highlights the **scarcity** of **spectrum** and the **high cost** of acquiring it.

2. Spectrum Interference and Coordination

2.1 Interference Between Services

One of the major challenges in spectrum allocation is avoiding **interference** between different services that use the same or adjacent frequencies. Without proper **coordination**, interference can result in poor network performance, dropped calls, or even complete service outages.

- **Adjacent Channel Interference**: 5G and other wireless services like **Wi-Fi**, **broadcasting**, and **military communications** can suffer from interference if they are assigned **overlapping or adjacent frequency bands**. For example, a **5G network** operating in the **3.5 GHz** band might interfere with **satellite communications** if proper **guard bands** (unused frequencies) aren't allocated between them.
- **Cross-Border Interference**: Radio signals do not respect national borders, so countries must work together to ensure that **5G networks** don't interfere with **networks** in neighboring regions. This is especially important for **high-frequency bands** like **mmWave**, which can travel long distances and affect networks in neighboring countries.

2.2 Global Coordination

While **national regulators** are responsible for managing spectrum within their borders, **global coordination** is essential to ensure the **harmonization of frequency bands**. The **ITU** (International Telecommunication Union) plays a central role in coordinating global spectrum management to minimize interference and ensure that frequencies are used efficiently.

- **Regional Spectrum Allocation**: Organizations like **ETSI** (European Telecommunications Standards Institute) and **3GPP** (3rd Generation Partnership Project) help harmonize spectrum usage across regions, ensuring that **5G networks** can operate seamlessly across borders.
- **International Agreements**: Countries must agree on which frequency bands can be used for **5G**, and which will be preserved for other uses (such as **satellite communications** or **broadcasting**). This is a time-consuming and complex process that requires international cooperation.

Practical Example:
During the **WRC-19** (World Radiocommunication Conference) held by the **ITU**, **countries worldwide** agreed to **harmonize** the use of **3.5 GHz** and **26 GHz** bands for **5G** deployment. This global agreement helped avoid interference and set the stage for **coordinated 5G deployment** across different countries.

---

3. Spectrum Auctions and Costs

3.1 The High Cost of Spectrum

Spectrum auctions have become the primary method for allocating spectrum to telecom operators. These auctions are often highly competitive and can raise substantial amounts of revenue for governments. For example, **5G spectrum auctions** in **the US**, **Europe**, and **Asia** have raised **billions of dollars**.

However, these **high costs** create challenges for telecom providers, particularly for smaller companies or those operating in emerging markets.

The **high price of spectrum** often leads to increased costs for **consumers**, as telecom companies pass on the expense of acquiring spectrum to their customers through **higher service fees**.

- **Limited Availability**: The limited supply of spectrum means that operators must often **compete fiercely** for the rights to use key frequency bands. This can limit the number of players in a market, reducing competition and potentially leading to higher prices for consumers.
- **Auction Complexity**: Spectrum auctions can be **complex** and **opaque**, with rules and bidding processes that vary from country to country. Telecom operators must be well-prepared to participate in these auctions, which can be resource-intensive.

3.2 Spectrum Reallocation

As **older wireless technologies** (like **2G** and **3G**) are phased out, regulators often look to **reallocate** spectrum to **5G** networks. This process is not always straightforward, as existing services may be using the same frequencies, leading to conflicts.

- **Relocation of Legacy Services**: For example, the **2G** and **3G** **networks** are being shut down in many countries to make room for **5G** services. However, this requires careful planning to ensure that existing users aren't left without service during the transition.
- **Shared Spectrum**: **Dynamic Spectrum Sharing (DSS)** is one way to address this challenge. DSS allows **4G** and **5G** networks to share the same spectrum in real-time, which can maximize the use of available spectrum without requiring **complete reallocation**.

Practical Example:
In the **UK**, the **Ofcom** regulatory body has been reallocating the **700 MHz band** (previously used for **TV broadcasting**) to **5G use**. This reallocation involved ensuring that the transition from broadcasting to mobile use was smooth, requiring careful planning to avoid disrupting **TV services** during the switch.

4. The Complexity of National vs. Global Interests

4.1 National Interests and Sovereignty

Each country has its own unique needs when it comes to **spectrum management**. For example, a country with **dense urban areas** may prioritize **high-frequency spectrum** for **5G**, while a country with **vast rural areas** may focus more on **low-band spectrum** to ensure **wide coverage**.

- **Balancing National Needs**: Governments must balance the desire to foster **advanced communications technologies** (like **5G**) with the need to preserve **spectrum** for other critical services like **military operations**, **weather satellites**, and **air traffic control**. The **spectrum allocation process** often requires making tough trade-offs between these competing demands.

4.2 The Risk of Fragmented Spectrum Markets

As **5G spectrum** is allocated, some regions may adopt different approaches to spectrum bands, which could lead to **fragmentation** in global markets. This can make it more difficult for telecom operators to offer **global roaming** services or for manufacturers to create devices that work seamlessly in different regions.

- **Inconsistent Spectrum Allocation**: For example, **Europe** and **North America** may allocate different portions of the **3.5 GHz** band for **5G use**, which could result in **incompatibility** between devices in the two regions. Similarly, **mmWave spectrum** may be available in some countries but not others, creating inconsistencies in network capabilities across borders.

Practical Example:
When traveling from **Europe** to **the US**, a **5G-enabled phone** may work seamlessly in one region but fail to connect to **5G networks** in the other due to differences in **spectrum bands**. This makes **global interoperability** an important challenge for **5G adoption**.

Navigating the Spectrum Allocation Challenges

The **challenges in spectrum allocation** are multifaceted, involving everything from **scarcity** and **high costs** to **international coordination** and **balancing national interests**. Efficiently managing the **radio frequency spectrum** is critical to ensuring the success of **5G networks**, enabling everything from **high-speed internet** and **autonomous driving** to **smart cities** and **massive IoT deployments**.

While **global organizations** like the **ITU** provide a framework for **coordinated spectrum management**, the process remains complex and requires ongoing negotiation and cooperation between **governments, telecom operators**, and **consumers**. As the demand for **5G services** grows, solving these challenges will be key to unlocking the full potential of **5G** and ensuring that the spectrum is used efficiently and fairly across the globe.

Chapter 9: Security in 5G Networks

With the deployment of **5G networks**, we are entering an era of unprecedented connectivity. The promise of **5G** lies in its ability to connect **millions of devices**, enabling everything from **smart cities** and **autonomous vehicles** to **healthcare innovations** and **industry 4.0**. However, with these new possibilities come new risks and vulnerabilities. The complexity of **5G networks**, combined with the vast number of connected devices, introduces new **cybersecurity threats** and challenges that need to be addressed to ensure the security and integrity of these networks.

9.1 Cybersecurity Risks and Threats in 5G

The rollout of **5G networks** promises significant advances in speed, latency, and connectivity, enabling the world to become more **hyper-connected** than ever before. However, these same capabilities also introduce new **cybersecurity risks** and **threats**. As **5G** expands its presence globally, it brings with it a broader attack surface for cybercriminals, state-sponsored actors, and other malicious entities.

---

1. Expanded Attack Surface and Increased Complexity

1.1 A More Complex Network Architecture

One of the defining features of **5G** is its **complex, decentralized architecture**. Unlike **4G**, which relies on a centralized network, **5G networks** are designed to be more **distributed**, using technologies like **small cells**, **edge computing**, and **network slicing**. This decentralized approach is essential for meeting the performance demands of **5G**, but it also introduces new points of vulnerability.

- **Small Cells**: **5G** relies on **small cell networks**, which are compact base stations deployed in dense urban areas, on streetlights, rooftops, and even within buildings. While **small cells** help with network **coverage** and **capacity**, their decentralized nature means they can be harder to secure. **Malicious actors** could potentially target these cells, causing localized disruptions or gaining access to sensitive data.
- **Edge Computing**: **Edge computing** brings computing resources closer to the **user**, reducing latency and improving performance. However, it also distributes **computational workloads** across a wider range of nodes, each of which could become a target for attackers. If one **edge server** is compromised, it can give attackers a **backdoor** into larger parts of the network.
- **Network Slicing**: One of the most innovative features of **5G** is **network slicing**, which divides the network into isolated, virtual segments (or "slices"), each dedicated to a specific use case, such as **autonomous vehicles**, **IoT**, or **massive data transfer**. While **network slicing** allows for customized services, it also creates new vulnerabilities because each slice must be securely isolated from others to prevent unauthorized access.

1.2 Increased Number of Connected Devices

The **5G network** is expected to support billions of **connected devices**, from **smartphones** and **wearables** to **industrial IoT** devices and **autonomous vehicles**. With so many devices continuously connected to the network, each device becomes a potential point of entry for attackers.

- **IoT Vulnerabilities**: Many **IoT devices** have weak or outdated security protocols, making them easy targets for hackers. Once compromised, an IoT device can serve as an entry point into a larger **5G network**, allowing attackers to move laterally and escalate their privileges. This is especially concerning for **critical infrastructure**, such as **smart grids** and **healthcare networks**, where vulnerabilities could have severe consequences.
- **Botnets and DDoS Attacks**: **5G** will facilitate the rise of **massive IoT networks**, potentially leading to the creation of large **botnets** used for **Distributed Denial-of-Service (DDoS)** attacks. With millions of devices connected to **5G networks**, attackers can create a **botnet** capable of overwhelming servers, causing outages or degrading the performance of the entire network.

Practical Example:
In 2016, the **Mirai botnet**, which compromised thousands of **IoT devices** such as **cameras** and **home routers**, was used to launch one of the **largest DDoS attacks** in history, targeting major websites like **Twitter**, **Netflix**, and **Spotify**. As **5G** accelerates the proliferation of **IoT devices**, similar threats could become even more common, affecting critical infrastructure and service availability.

---

2. Potential Cybersecurity Threats in 5G Networks

2.1 Denial-of-Service (DoS) and Distributed Denial-of-Service (DDoS) Attacks

DoS and **DDoS** attacks are already prevalent in **cybersecurity**, and **5G** networks are at risk of these threats being amplified due to their larger attack surface and the **increased number of connected devices**.

- **5G's Distributed Nature**: Because **5G** networks rely on a more distributed architecture with **small cells** and **edge computing**, attackers can target vulnerable parts of the network with greater ease. **DDoS attacks** could target these distributed nodes, causing widespread service disruptions.
- **Impact of DDoS on 5G**: The effects of a **DDoS attack** on a **5G network** could be catastrophic. In a **smart city**, for example, a **DDoS attack** could overwhelm **5G network resources**, disrupting critical services like **traffic management**, **healthcare services**, or **security systems**.

Practical Example:
In **2018**, the **GitHub platform** experienced one of the largest **DDoS attacks** ever recorded, peaking at **1.35 Tbps**. This was a **reflection-based DDoS** attack that flooded the platform with more traffic than it could handle. Given the increased reliance on **cloud services** and **edge computing** in **5G**, the risk of such attacks intensifies.

2.2 Data Breaches and Interception

With **5G** supporting higher data speeds and greater bandwidth, the volume of sensitive data transferred over these networks is expected to increase substantially. This presents a major challenge for **data protection**.

- **Man-in-the-Middle (MitM) Attacks**: A **Man-in-the-Middle** attack occurs when an attacker intercepts and potentially alters the communication between two parties without their knowledge. While **5G** incorporates stronger encryption and security measures, the sheer volume of data transmitted and the expanded network architecture present new opportunities for attackers to target vulnerable connections and intercept sensitive data.
- **Mobile Malware**: As **5G** enables faster speeds and greater connectivity, **malware** could spread more easily through the network. This could include malicious apps that steal personal data or disrupt the normal operation of devices connected to the **5G network**.

Practical Example:
In 2017, **Equifax**, a major credit reporting agency, suffered a massive data breach in which hackers exploited a vulnerability in their web server software to steal sensitive data, including personal information from **143 million Americans**. With **5G** supporting more interconnected devices, the potential for **data breaches** is likely to increase if devices aren't properly secured.

3. Addressing Cybersecurity Risks in 5G Networks

3.1 Network-Level Security Measures

- **Encryption**: End-to-end **encryption** will be crucial in protecting sensitive data from being intercepted during transmission. **5G networks** should implement strong encryption protocols, such as **TLS** and **IPsec**, to safeguard both **user data** and **network communications**.
- **Zero Trust Architecture**: Given the distributed nature of **5G**, implementing a **Zero Trust Architecture** (ZTA) is vital. In a **Zero Trust model**, every device or user is considered untrusted until proven otherwise. This means that authentication,

authorization, and encryption are required for **every transaction** on the network, regardless of the source or destination.

- **Network Slicing Security**: Each **network slice** in **5G** should be independently secured. **Access control** mechanisms, **firewalls**, and **encryption** should be implemented to ensure that no slice can compromise the others. A dedicated **security slice** can be used for **critical services** like **autonomous vehicles** or **remote surgery**, which require **higher security** than standard applications.

Practical Example:
In **Germany**, **Deutsche Telekom** has implemented **network slicing** to isolate different types of traffic, including **critical communications** for **industrial IoT** devices and **autonomous vehicles**. This segmentation improves security by ensuring that **sensitive communications** are kept isolated from less critical traffic, reducing the risk of cross-slice attacks.

3.2 Securing IoT Devices and the Edge

The rapid expansion of **IoT devices** connected to **5G** requires heightened attention to their **security**.

- **Device Authentication**: **IoT devices** must use strong **authentication mechanisms** to ensure they cannot be hijacked. This includes the use of **public key infrastructure (PKI)** and **multi-factor authentication (MFA)** for IoT devices.
- **Edge Computing Security**: Since **edge computing** brings computation closer to the user, it becomes critical to secure **edge nodes** and **data centers** that handle sensitive data. **AI-based security solutions** can help monitor and protect these nodes from potential cyber threats in real time.

Practical Example:
In **China**, a **smart city** infrastructure implemented **advanced encryption** and **identity-based access control** for IoT devices and edge nodes. This helps to ensure that even if one device is compromised, it cannot compromise the entire city's infrastructure.

3.3 Continuous Monitoring and Incident Response

As **5G networks** grow more complex, **continuous monitoring** of network traffic is essential to detect and respond to emerging threats.

- **AI-Powered Security**: Artificial **intelligence (AI)** can be used to monitor network traffic and detect anomalous behavior in real time. **Machine learning** algorithms can identify potential threats, such as **DDoS attacks** or **data breaches**, and trigger automated responses to mitigate the impact.
- **Incident Response Plans**: Operators should have robust **incident response plans** in place. This includes **backup systems**, **network isolation protocols**, and regular **security audits** to ensure that if a breach does occur, the impact is minimized.

Building a Secure Future for 5G

As the world transitions to **5G**, ensuring **cybersecurity** is paramount. The expanded **attack surface**, the proliferation of **IoT devices**, and the **distributed architecture** of **5G** present new challenges in maintaining a secure network. However, by implementing **strong encryption**, **Zero Trust** models, **network slicing security**, and **continuous monitoring**, operators can significantly mitigate the risks associated with **5G networks**.

The **cybersecurity** of **5G** is a shared responsibility between **telecom operators**, **device manufacturers**, and **governments**. As **5G networks** continue to evolve, ongoing vigilance, collaboration, and innovation will be essential in safeguarding the network and ensuring that the **digital future** remains secure for all users.

9.2 Securing Data in a Hyper-Connected World

As **5G networks** continue to expand and **connect** an ever-growing number of devices, we are entering an era where **data** is being generated, transferred, and stored at unprecedented rates. The ability to securely protect that data—whether it's **personal information**, **financial records**, or **critical infrastructure data**—is now more important than ever. In the age of **hyper-connectivity**, **data security** becomes a **fundamental pillar** for ensuring that the promise of **5G**—enabling everything from **smart cities** to **autonomous vehicles**—is realized safely and responsibly.

---

1. The Hyper-Connected World and Data Explosion

1.1 The Impact of Hyper-Connectivity

With **5G networks** promising to connect everything from **smartphones** to **wearables**, **industrial machines**, and even **autonomous cars**, the volume of data being generated is exploding. By 2025, it is expected that **5G networks** will connect over **25 billion devices** globally, all transmitting data at incredibly high speeds. This increase in connected devices presents **new opportunities** but also **new risks** related to the collection, processing, and storage of sensitive information.

- **IoT Devices**: **5G** will enable billions of **IoT devices**, such as **health trackers**, **smart appliances**, **industrial sensors**, and **connected vehicles**, all collecting and transmitting data continuously. These devices can often have **weak security**, making them vulnerable to cyber-attacks.
- **Massive Data Streams**: The continuous generation of data requires **real-time analysis** and **secure transmission**, which makes it increasingly difficult to protect sensitive information from threats like **data interception** and **malware**.

1.2 Data in Transit and At Rest

In a **5G world**, **data** will be transmitted over vast distances and stored in numerous locations, both **on-premise** and in the **cloud**. The following scenarios illustrate the complexity of securing this data:

- **Data in Transit**: As data travels from one device to another over the **5G network**, it's vulnerable to interception or alteration by attackers. Ensuring **confidentiality** and **integrity** during transmission is a critical aspect of data security.
- **Data at Rest**: Even when data is stored (in **databases**, **cloud services**, or **edge devices**), it must be securely protected from unauthorized access. Whether it's **personal health data**, **financial**

information, or **industrial control data**, securing data at rest is just as crucial as protecting it during transmission.

Practical Example:
In **smart cities**, **data** from **traffic sensors**, **public Wi-Fi**, and **environmental monitoring devices** is transmitted through the **5G network**. Securing this data during transmission and ensuring that it is stored securely in **cloud data centers** is essential for maintaining privacy and preventing data breaches.

---

2. Key Approaches to Securing Data in 5G Networks

2.1 Encryption: The Cornerstone of Data Protection

Encryption is the most fundamental and effective way to protect **data** in a **5G** environment, whether it's **data in transit** or **data at rest**. Encryption transforms **plaintext data** into a scrambled format that can only be understood by those with the correct decryption key.

- **End-to-End Encryption**: With **5G**, **end-to-end encryption** is crucial to ensure that data is **encrypted** at the sender's side and **decrypted** only at the receiver's end. This means that even if **data packets** are intercepted, they cannot be read or tampered with.
- **Transport Layer Security (TLS)**: **TLS** is the standard encryption protocol for securing **internet traffic**. It's commonly used to protect data during transmission across **5G networks**. **5G operators** and **service providers** should implement strong **TLS** encryption for all data that travels over public networks.
- **Encryption of Data at Rest**: When data is stored on a device or in the cloud, it must be encrypted to prevent unauthorized access. This is especially important for sensitive **healthcare data** or **financial records**, where **unauthorized access** can lead to severe consequences.

Practical Example:
To secure **personal health data** in a **telemedicine application**, healthcare providers use **end-to-end encryption** to ensure that patient data is encrypted when sent from the **patient's device** to the **healthcare**

provider's system. Even if a hacker intercepts the data during transmission, they cannot read it without the decryption key.

2.2 Access Control: Limiting Who Can Access Data

Managing who has access to **sensitive data** is an essential part of securing it. Implementing strong **access control** measures ensures that only authorized individuals or devices can access critical data.

- **Authentication**: One of the first lines of defense in **access control** is **authentication**. This involves verifying the identity of a user or device before granting access to the network. In **5G**, it's important to use **multi-factor authentication (MFA)**, which combines two or more verification methods (e.g., passwords, biometrics, smart cards).
- **Role-Based Access Control (RBAC)**: **RBAC** is a method where users are granted access based on their role within an organization. For example, a **network administrator** may have access to all **5G network components**, while an **end user** may only be able to access certain applications or services.
- **Device Authentication**: With **5G** enabling a vast array of connected **IoT devices**, authenticating devices before they can communicate over the network is critical. Each device must have a **unique identifier**, and only **trusted devices** should be allowed to interact with the network.

Practical Example:
In a **smart factory**, only authorized **factory managers** and **maintenance personnel** should have access to **sensitive machine data**. By using **RBAC**, the system ensures that only these roles can interact with the control systems, while other employees are restricted to lower-level functions.

2.3 Secure Data Storage and Backup

Storing data securely in the **cloud** or on **edge devices** is essential to protect it from **unauthorized access** or **data breaches**. Secure data storage should include **encryption, regular backups**, and **access control mechanisms**.

- **Cloud Security**: Since much of the **5G** ecosystem is built on **cloud computing**, it's crucial to ensure that data stored in the cloud is properly **encrypted** and that the **cloud provider** has strong **security measures** in place.
- **Data Redundancy and Backup**: In case of a **security breach** or **data loss**, organizations must have **redundant data storage** and a **backup plan** to recover the data. This could involve **replicating data** across multiple geographic locations or using **hybrid cloud** solutions that combine on-premise and cloud-based backups.

Practical Example:
In a **smart city**, data collected from **traffic sensors** and **surveillance cameras** is stored securely in the **cloud**. The data is **encrypted** and replicated across **multiple data centers** to ensure it is always available for analysis, even if one server or data center fails.

---

3. Data Privacy in 5G: Ensuring User Rights and Compliance

As the volume of **personal data** handled by **5G networks** grows, it's crucial to ensure **data privacy** and compliance with **regulations** like the **General Data Protection Regulation (GDPR)** and **California Consumer Privacy Act (CCPA)**.

3.1 Data Minimization and User Consent

- **Data Minimization**: In line with **GDPR** principles, **5G networks** should follow **data minimization** principles, meaning only the **minimum amount of personal data** necessary for a service should be collected. This reduces the risk of **data exposure** or misuse.
- **User Consent**: **5G operators** must ensure that users are **fully informed** about what data is being collected and how it will be used. Obtaining **explicit consent** from users is crucial, especially when collecting sensitive data such as **health information** or **location data**.

3.2 Regulatory Compliance

- **GDPR and Other Regulations**: 5G networks must comply with global privacy regulations like the **GDPR** in Europe or the **CCPA** in California. This includes **providing users with rights** to access, rectify, or delete their personal data and ensuring that data is stored and processed according to the highest privacy standards.

Practical Example:
A **5G healthcare app** that collects **patient data** must ensure compliance with **HIPAA** (Health Insurance Portability and Accountability Act) in the United States. This includes **encryption** of health data, ensuring patient consent for data sharing, and providing patients with access to their health data upon request.

4. Securing 5G Data: A Shared Responsibility

Securing data in a **hyper-connected world** requires a **shared responsibility** between **telecom providers**, **device manufacturers**, **service providers**, and **regulatory bodies**. It's not enough to rely on a single entity to secure data; instead, **everyone** in the **5G ecosystem** must adhere to **best practices** and work collaboratively to ensure the safety and privacy of data.

4.1 Collaboration Across Sectors

- **Telecom Providers**: Operators must ensure that **5G networks** are built with **strong security frameworks**, including **encryption**, **access control**, and **traffic monitoring**. They must also ensure **secure network slices** for different use cases, such as **autonomous vehicles** or **healthcare services**.
- **Device Manufacturers**: **IoT device manufacturers** must design devices with **built-in security features**, such as **strong authentication** and **secure firmware**. Devices should also be upgradable so they can receive **security patches** as vulnerabilities are discovered.
- **Governments and Regulators**: Governments must create and enforce **data protection** and **privacy regulations** that ensure telecom operators and service providers comply with security standards.

Practical Example:
The **UK's National Cyber Security Centre (NCSC)** works with telecom companies to improve the **security of 5G networks** by providing guidelines and best practices for operators and suppliers. These guidelines include **security controls** for **small cells, network equipment**, and **5G core infrastructure**.

Ensuring a Secure 5G Future

Securing data in a **hyper-connected world** enabled by **5G** is a complex but essential task. With billions of devices connected, **5G networks** must be designed with robust **encryption, access control**, and **data privacy** practices to ensure the security of both **users** and **critical infrastructure**.

9.3 Future-Proofing 5G: Privacy and Regulatory Measures

The **5G era** marks the beginning of a more interconnected world, where everything from **smart homes** and **wearables** to **autonomous vehicles** and **industrial IoT systems** will rely on high-speed, low-latency connections. While the potential benefits of **5G** are vast, there are substantial privacy and regulatory challenges that must be addressed to ensure that these new technologies are deployed securely and responsibly.

As **5G networks** continue to expand, ensuring the **privacy** of users and the **security of data** becomes a priority. Governments, telecom providers, device manufacturers, and consumers all play key roles in safeguarding **data privacy** and complying with **regulations** that will govern **5G networks**.

1. Privacy in the 5G World

With the massive **increase in connected devices** and the **vast amounts of data** being transmitted through **5G networks**, privacy becomes a significant concern. The amount of **personal data** shared by devices—such as **location**, **health metrics**, and **behavioral data**—opens up new opportunities for **tracking**, **profiling**, and potential misuse.

1.1 The Privacy Challenges of 5G Networks

- **Location Tracking**: **5G networks** enable **precise location tracking** through **small cells** and **beamforming** technology. While this can benefit services like **location-based marketing** or **navigation**, it also raises concerns about **tracking** individuals without their consent.
- **Data Harvesting**: The sheer number of connected devices—from **smart home devices** to **wearables**—means that **vast amounts of personal data** are constantly being collected and transmitted. Ensuring that **consumers** are aware of and can control the **data harvesting** processes is crucial to maintaining trust.
- **Data Sharing Across Platforms**: **5G networks** facilitate **cross-platform data sharing**, meaning data may flow between telecom providers, cloud services, third-party apps, and other organizations. This creates complexities around **who owns the data**, **who has access to it**, and how it is **protected**.

1.2 Privacy-Enhancing Technologies (PETs)

As **5G** enables more personalized services, there is an urgent need to incorporate **privacy-enhancing technologies (PETs)** into **5G networks** to mitigate these risks.

- **End-to-End Encryption**: Ensuring that **data in transit** is encrypted end-to-end is one of the best ways to secure user privacy. Even if data is intercepted, it will be unreadable to unauthorized parties.
- **Anonymization and Pseudonymization**: Techniques like **data anonymization** (removing personally identifiable information) and **pseudonymization** (replacing personal identifiers with pseudonyms) can help protect users' identities while still allowing for data analysis and service delivery.
- **Zero Knowledge Proofs**: A cutting-edge cryptographic technique that allows a user to prove they know certain information (such as

a password or key) without revealing the actual data. This is increasingly important for ensuring that sensitive data remains secure during verification processes.

Practical Example:
Apple and **Google** have implemented **end-to-end encryption** for **iMessages** and **Google Hangouts**. This ensures that messages sent between users are not accessible to anyone except the recipients, protecting sensitive communication from unauthorized access.

2. Regulatory Measures for 5G Privacy

As **5G networks** grow, regulators will need to develop frameworks that balance the demands of **innovation** and **privacy protection**. These frameworks must not only protect consumers' privacy but also ensure that **telecom providers** and **device manufacturers** adhere to strict data protection standards.

2.1 Privacy Regulations Around the World

- **General Data Protection Regulation (GDPR)**: GDPR, introduced in 2018 by the **European Union**, is one of the most robust privacy regulations to date. It mandates that **organizations** must obtain **explicit consent** from users to collect personal data and allows users the right to request their data be deleted or corrected.
  - For **5G networks**, **GDPR compliance** means ensuring that **users' consent** is obtained for the collection of data and that **data minimization** principles are followed (only collecting necessary data).
  - It also introduces the **right to be forgotten**, meaning consumers can request the deletion of their data from all systems.
- **California Consumer Privacy Act (CCPA)**: CCPA, which became effective in 2020, grants **California residents** the right to access, delete, and opt out of the sale of their personal information. **5G operators** and **service providers** in the **US** must ensure they comply with **CCPA** by informing consumers of what data is being

collected and offering them the ability to control how their data is used.

- **Personal Data Protection Bill (India)**: India's **Personal Data Protection Bill**, introduced in 2019, seeks to strengthen data privacy rights for Indian citizens. Under this bill, **telecom operators** must store **sensitive personal data** only in India, and citizens have the right to access their personal data stored by **telecom companies**.

2.2 Impact of Privacy Laws on 5G Deployment

Regulatory frameworks like **GDPR** and **CCPA** place a significant burden on **telecom operators** and **service providers** to protect consumer data. For **5G networks** to comply with these laws:

- **Data Transparency**: **Consumers** must be informed about **what data is being collected, why it's being collected**, and **how it will be used**.
- **Informed Consent**: **Telecom operators** must obtain **explicit consent** from users before collecting their data. This could involve having users agree to clear, easy-to-understand privacy policies before connecting to a **5G network**.
- **Data Portability**: Many privacy regulations require **data portability**, meaning users can transfer their personal data from one service provider to another. This is particularly important as users move from one **5G service provider** to another.

Practical Example:
Under **GDPR**, when a **5G operator** collects **location data** from users for services like **traffic management** or **location-based advertising**, it must ensure that users are **informed** about the data collection process and give **explicit consent**. If users decide to withdraw their consent, they must be able to **easily opt out** and have their data deleted.

---

3. Ensuring Long-Term Security and Privacy for 5G Networks

3.1 Adapting to Emerging Privacy Threats

The dynamic nature of **5G networks** requires that privacy measures evolve to keep up with emerging threats. As the **number of connected devices** continues to grow, cybercriminals will develop increasingly sophisticated attack techniques. Future-proofing **5G privacy** will require the continuous adaptation of **security practices** and **data protection strategies**.

- **Quantum-Resistant Cryptography**: One of the greatest emerging threats to **5G privacy** is the advent of **quantum computing**. While **quantum computers** are not yet widely available, they could eventually be capable of breaking current **encryption** methods. Therefore, it's essential to explore **quantum-resistant encryption** methods that will remain secure even in the era of quantum computing.
- **AI-Driven Security**: **AI** and **machine learning** can play an essential role in identifying **new privacy risks** in real-time. By continuously monitoring network traffic and user behavior, **AI-driven security tools** can detect anomalies or potential threats before they cause significant damage.

3.2 Collaborative Efforts Between Governments, Operators, and Consumers

The implementation of **privacy measures** in **5G networks** is a shared responsibility between **governments**, **telecom operators**, and **consumers**. Governments must establish strong regulatory frameworks, telecom operators must adhere to privacy standards, and consumers must understand and protect their privacy rights.

- **Public Awareness**: Consumers need to be **educated** about their **data rights** in the **5G era**. Governments and operators should invest in **public awareness campaigns** that explain how personal data is collected, stored, and used within **5G networks**.
- **Security Standards**: Governments and **industry bodies** must work together to develop **unified security standards** that all operators can follow. This ensures consistency in **5G security** and **data protection** practices across regions and providers.

Practical Example:
In **Japan**, the **Ministry of Internal Affairs and Communications** has partnered with **telecom companies** to introduce **secure 5G services** that

ensure consumer privacy is maintained. These efforts include **regular audits** of network security and **privacy practices** to ensure compliance with national laws.

Future-Proofing 5G Privacy and Security

As **5G networks** continue to expand and play a larger role in everyday life, ensuring **privacy** and **data protection** will be critical to maintaining trust and security. Governments, **telecom operators**, and consumers all have roles to play in future-proofing **5G networks** against emerging threats and ensuring that privacy regulations evolve to meet the demands of new technologies.

Part 4: Advanced Use Cases and Industry Applications

Chapter 10: 5G in Healthcare and Telemedicine

The **5G network** has the potential to revolutionize **healthcare** by enabling faster, more reliable, and secure communications across a wide range of medical services. From **remote surgeries** to **real-time patient monitoring** and **telehealth services**, **5G** is paving the way for a more connected and efficient healthcare system. This chapter delves into how **5G** is transforming the healthcare landscape and the opportunities and challenges it presents for **telemedicine** and **healthcare management**.

10.1 Remote Surgeries and Real-Time Patient Monitoring

As the world of **healthcare** continues to evolve, **5G technology** is playing a pivotal role in transforming how medical services are delivered. **Remote surgeries** and **real-time patient monitoring** are two areas that are being revolutionized by **5G**, offering the potential to improve healthcare accessibility, quality, and efficiency.

1. Remote Surgeries: Performing Surgeries from a Distance

Imagine a world where a **top-tier surgeon** in **New York** can assist in or even **perform surgery** on a patient in **rural Africa**, with no significant time delay or loss of precision. This is the promise of **remote surgery** powered by **5G networks**. **5G's ultra-low latency**, **high data rates**, and **high reliability** enable surgeons to perform procedures with **real-time control** of **robotic surgical instruments**, regardless of the physical distance between them and the patient.

1.1 How 5G Enables Remote Surgeries

- **Low Latency**: The most critical requirement for **remote surgeries** is **low latency**—the delay between a surgeon's actions and the response of the robotic instruments. **5G's latency** is as low as **1 millisecond**, which is crucial for precision surgery. A delay of even a few seconds can result in serious complications, but with **5G**, surgeons can control robotic arms or tools in **real-time** with near-zero delay.
- **High-Speed Data Transmission**: Remote surgeries require high-resolution **video feeds** and **data transmission** from medical imaging equipment like **scanners** or **X-rays**. **5G's high bandwidth** allows these large data files to be transferred seamlessly between the surgeon's console and the operating room, ensuring that the surgeon has a clear and accurate view of the operation.
- **Real-Time Haptic Feedback**: One of the challenges of performing surgery remotely is the lack of **physical touch** or **tactile feedback**. In traditional surgeries, surgeons rely on their sense of touch to guide their actions. With **5G**, **haptic feedback** technology allows the surgeon to "feel" the surgery through **robotic instruments**. This feedback is transmitted in real-time via the **5G network**, enhancing the surgeon's control during the procedure.

Practical Example:
In **2020**, a landmark **5G-powered remote surgery** was conducted in **China**, where a surgeon in **Beijing** used **5G technology** to control a **robotic surgical system** during **spinal surgery** on a patient in **Sichuan**, located **30 kilometers away**. The surgery was successful, demonstrating the potential for **remote surgeries** to extend expert medical care to underserved areas.

1.2 Benefits of Remote Surgeries

- **Access to Expert Care**: **5G-enabled remote surgeries** can bring **specialized care** to remote or underserved areas. **Rural areas** often suffer from a lack of skilled surgeons, but **5G networks** can bridge this gap, allowing patients to receive care from the best surgeons, regardless of their geographical location.
- **Reduced Travel Time**: Patients no longer need to travel long distances to receive complex surgical treatments. This is

particularly beneficial for those in **rural** or **developing regions** where **medical facilities** may be scarce.

- **Cost Efficiency**: Remote surgeries can reduce the costs associated with patient transportation and hospital stays. Surgeons can perform multiple surgeries remotely in different locations, thus reducing operational costs in **hospitals** and clinics.

1.3 Challenges and Considerations

- **Infrastructure Requirements**: Implementing **remote surgeries** on a wide scale requires robust **5G infrastructure**. In many rural or underserved areas, the necessary infrastructure to support **5G networks** might not be in place, which could limit the availability of this service.
- **Surgeon Training**: Surgeons need to be trained in using **robotic systems** and **remote surgery techniques**, as operating remotely requires not only technical expertise but also proficiency in controlling robotic tools through a screen with minimal tactile feedback.
- **Security Concerns**: The **cybersecurity** of remote surgeries is of paramount importance. Surgeons and healthcare institutions must ensure that the data transmitted during the surgery is encrypted, and the communication systems are secure to prevent hacking or data breaches.

---

2. Real-Time Patient Monitoring: Keeping Track of Patients Anywhere, Anytime

In addition to **remote surgeries**, **5G** is enabling **real-time patient monitoring**, where healthcare professionals can continuously track patients' **vital signs**, **health conditions**, and **treatment progress**. This technology is particularly useful in managing **chronic conditions** and providing care to patients who cannot physically visit healthcare facilities.

2.1 How 5G Enables Real-Time Patient Monitoring

- **Continuous Data Transmission**: With **5G**, patient data can be transmitted continuously from wearable devices or **smart sensors** to healthcare providers. These devices monitor **heart rate**, **blood**

pressure, **blood sugar levels**, **oxygen saturation**, and other critical health parameters. With **5G's low latency**, this data is sent in **real-time**, allowing for immediate response from healthcare providers.

- **Wearable Devices**: **5G-enabled wearables**, such as **smartwatches** and **biosensors**, can transmit a **steady stream of health data** directly to healthcare systems. These devices are constantly collecting data, which can be analyzed by **AI systems** to detect abnormalities or predict potential health crises before they occur.
- **Telemonitoring Systems**: **Telemonitoring** systems can use **5G technology** to collect and analyze data remotely, allowing **doctors** to monitor their patients from anywhere in the world. These systems can send alerts if a patient's condition changes, ensuring that healthcare professionals are always aware of any emerging issues.

Practical Example:
Verily, a subsidiary of **Alphabet (Google's parent company)**, is developing a **5G-enabled healthcare system** that uses **wearable devices** to continuously monitor **chronic conditions** like **diabetes**. The system not only tracks **blood sugar levels** but also sends data to **healthcare providers** in **real-time**, allowing them to adjust treatment plans based on up-to-date information.

2.2 Benefits of Real-Time Patient Monitoring

- **Immediate Medical Response**: Real-time data allows healthcare providers to respond instantly to changes in a patient's condition. This can be life-saving in cases of **heart attacks**, **stroke**, or **diabetic crises** when **every second counts**.
- **Chronic Disease Management**: For patients with **chronic conditions** such as **hypertension**, **asthma**, or **heart disease**, continuous monitoring helps doctors track the progression of the disease and adjust treatment plans in real-time, improving patient outcomes.
- **Reduced Hospital Visits**: With continuous remote monitoring, patients can avoid frequent visits to the hospital or clinic. This is particularly valuable for elderly patients or those with mobility issues who might find it challenging to travel to healthcare facilities.

2.3 Challenges of Real-Time Patient Monitoring

- **Data Privacy and Security**: As healthcare data is transmitted across networks, ensuring the **security** and **privacy** of this data is critical. Healthcare providers must ensure that all data transmitted from patient devices is **encrypted** and that proper **access controls** are in place.
- **Device Compatibility**: To ensure seamless monitoring, **5G-enabled devices** must be compatible with the various healthcare systems in use. Ensuring **interoperability** between different platforms and devices is an ongoing challenge for healthcare providers.
- **Cost of Technology**: While **5G** enables real-time patient monitoring, the cost of **wearable devices**, **sensors**, and **data analytics systems** can be prohibitive, especially in low-income regions or for patients without insurance coverage. Overcoming this barrier is essential to ensure that the technology is accessible to all patients.

3. The Future of Remote Surgeries and Real-Time Monitoring

The future of **remote surgeries** and **real-time patient monitoring** powered by **5G** is incredibly promising. As **5G infrastructure** continues to roll out globally, **remote surgeries** could become more common, bringing high-quality medical care to the most underserved regions. Likewise, **real-time patient monitoring** can make **chronic disease management** more efficient, reduce hospital readmission rates, and ultimately improve **patient outcomes**.

3.1 Innovations on the Horizon

- **AI Integration**: **Artificial intelligence** will play an increasingly important role in **analyzing patient data** from wearables and remote surgeries. AI algorithms can help doctors make faster, more accurate decisions by analyzing the continuous stream of patient data for **trends**, **patterns**, and **anomalies**.
- **Expanded Use of Robotic Surgery**: With **5G**, **robotic surgery** will become even more advanced, enabling more delicate and

164

complex procedures to be performed remotely. As **5G networks** expand, more hospitals will be able to leverage these technologies, providing **specialist-level care** in more locations.

Practical Example:
Intuitive Surgical's da Vinci system has already demonstrated the potential of **robotic surgery**, but **5G** will allow these systems to perform **more complex procedures** remotely. Surgeons in one country could collaborate on **highly technical surgeries**, improving the overall healthcare landscape and making expert care accessible globally.

5G technology is set to redefine the future of healthcare, particularly in the areas of **remote surgeries** and **real-time patient monitoring**. The ability to perform surgeries remotely and continuously monitor patients will make healthcare more **efficient, personalized**, and **accessible**. While challenges such as **data security**, **device compatibility**, and **cost** remain, the transformative potential of **5G** in healthcare is undeniable. The combination of **5G's speed, low latency**, and **high reliability** will open new doors for **medical practitioners** and **patients**, ultimately improving **outcomes** and **saving lives**.

10.2 The Role of 5G in Telehealth Services

The advent of **5G technology** is poised to transform many industries, and **telehealth** is one of the most significant beneficiaries. **Telehealth**—the delivery of healthcare services remotely using digital technology—has existed for years, but the **speed, low latency**, and **reliability** of **5G** will unlock new possibilities, making it more accessible, efficient, and effective than ever before.

1. The Rise of Telehealth

Telehealth is not a new concept, but it has gained widespread recognition due to its ability to increase access to healthcare, particularly in rural or underserved regions. **Telehealth services** have been integral in areas such as:

- **Virtual consultations** between doctors and patients
- **Remote monitoring** of chronic diseases
- **Mental health support** through teletherapy
- **Post-surgery care** or **follow-up consultations**

Before the widespread adoption of **5G**, **4G LTE** networks supported many of these services, but they came with limitations in terms of **latency** (delays in communication) and **bandwidth** (data capacity). **5G** overcomes these limitations, facilitating a more robust and seamless experience for both healthcare providers and patients.

---

2. How 5G Improves Telehealth Services

2.1 Real-Time Video Consultations

One of the most significant advantages of **5G** in **telehealth** is the ability to facilitate **real-time video consultations**. Whether for **routine check-ups**, **specialist consultations**, or **emergency care**, **5G** enhances the quality of video calls, ensuring **crystal-clear video quality** with **no latency**.

- **High-Definition Video**: With **5G's high data speeds**, healthcare providers can conduct **HD-quality video consultations**, which are essential for examining patients remotely. Doctors can observe **skin conditions**, **eye health**, and other visual symptoms that require high-resolution video to make accurate diagnoses.
- **Low Latency**: The low latency of **5G** (as low as **1 millisecond**) ensures **real-time interaction** with no delays, which is critical in **emergency consultations**, where every second counts. **5G's low latency** allows doctors and patients to interact naturally, making the consultation process more effective and engaging.
- **Increased Accessibility**: Rural patients who otherwise might not have access to **specialists** or **care facilities** can benefit from **5G-enabled telehealth consultations**, which bring high-quality care to

remote locations, cutting down the need for **travel** and **waiting times**.

Practical Example:
In **India**, **5G-enabled telehealth platforms** have been rolled out to allow rural populations to access **specialized healthcare** from **city-based doctors**. **5G-powered video consultations** have improved diagnostic accuracy and reduced the time required for medical professionals to treat patients in remote areas.

2.2 Remote Diagnostics

5G is facilitating the delivery of **remote diagnostics**, allowing healthcare providers to monitor patients' health in real-time using **connected medical devices**. These devices collect data such as **heart rate**, **blood pressure**, **temperature**, and **oxygen levels** and send it securely to healthcare providers for immediate analysis.

- **Real-Time Data Transmission**: With **5G's high bandwidth**, **large data packets**, such as high-resolution **CT scans** or **X-rays**, can be transmitted in real time to specialists for analysis. This is particularly useful in **tele-radiology** and **tele-pathology**, where large image files need to be analyzed remotely.
- **Wearables**: **5G-enabled wearable devices**, such as **smartwatches** and **biosensors**, continuously monitor **vital signs** and **chronic conditions**. For example, a **heart disease patient** can wear a **5G-enabled ECG monitor** that sends **heart data** to a healthcare provider, enabling them to monitor the patient's condition in real-time and intervene promptly if necessary.
- **Predictive Diagnostics**: **AI-powered systems** integrated with **5G** can analyze real-time data from remote diagnostics to predict medical conditions before they become critical. This can help identify health issues early, especially in **patients with chronic diseases**.

Practical Example:
In **South Korea**, **5G-enabled remote diagnostic systems** are used to monitor **patients with diabetes**. Wearable sensors track **blood glucose levels**, and **real-time data** is transmitted via **5G networks** to **healthcare providers**. If a patient's levels exceed safe thresholds, the system

immediately sends an **alert** to both the patient and their healthcare provider, enabling rapid intervention.

2.3 Remote Patient Monitoring

Continuous **remote patient monitoring** is one of the key applications of **5G** in **telehealth**. By integrating **5G networks** with **IoT devices**, healthcare providers can monitor **patients** in **real-time**, tracking various health metrics from home or in remote locations.

- **Chronic Disease Management**: **5G** enables continuous **monitoring** of chronic conditions such as **heart disease**, **hypertension**, and **asthma**. For example, a patient with **heart disease** might wear a **5G-enabled device** that tracks their **ECG readings** throughout the day and sends updates to the healthcare provider.
- **Enhanced Support for Elderly Patients**: Older adults with **mobility issues** or those who are **bedridden** benefit greatly from **remote monitoring**. Devices like **fall detection sensors** and **vital signs monitors** can immediately notify caregivers and healthcare providers about any significant changes in the patient's condition.
- **Home Healthcare**: With **5G**, healthcare providers can expand services like **home healthcare** and **nursing services** by remotely monitoring **patients' health metrics** through **connected devices**. This reduces the burden on hospitals and clinics while ensuring that patients continue to receive care in the comfort of their own homes.

Practical Example:
In **the United States**, **5G-powered remote monitoring systems** have been implemented in **home healthcare programs**. These systems track **vital signs**, such as **blood pressure** and **oxygen saturation**, and send data to healthcare providers. If a significant change is detected, **healthcare professionals** can adjust the care plan in real-time.

---

3. Benefits of 5G in Telehealth

3.1 Increased Access to Healthcare

One of the most significant benefits of **5G** in **telehealth** is the **increased access to healthcare** in underserved or remote areas. Patients in **rural** or **remote locations**, where medical professionals may be few or unavailable, can receive consultations from **specialist doctors** without the need to travel long distances.

- **Rural and Underserved Areas**: 5G's **high-speed connectivity** makes it feasible to extend telehealth services to regions that were previously too remote to support such services. In regions where access to **specialized care** is limited, **5G-powered telehealth** connects patients to the best care available.
- **Disaster Relief**: During natural disasters or crises where **traditional healthcare infrastructure** may be overwhelmed, **5G-enabled telehealth** systems can provide immediate **remote consultation** and **monitoring**.

3.2 Reduced Healthcare Costs

Telehealth powered by **5G** reduces **healthcare costs** by eliminating the need for **patients to travel**, reducing **hospital visits**, and streamlining the **administrative processes** involved in managing healthcare.

- **Cost Savings for Patients**: With **remote consultations**, patients don't have to spend money on transportation or **out-of-pocket healthcare costs** for visits to the doctor. This is especially beneficial for those living in **rural areas** or **developing countries**.
- **Operational Efficiency**: Healthcare providers can streamline their workflows by integrating **5G-enabled telehealth systems** for **remote monitoring**, **virtual consultations**, and **data sharing**. This reduces the burden on physical healthcare facilities and enhances service delivery efficiency.

Practical Example:
A **telehealth program** in **Brazil** has been using **5G to offer remote consultations** for **diabetic patients** in rural areas. The program has cut down **travel costs** for patients and improved **health outcomes**, as patients can now receive timely advice and care from specialists without needing to travel to a city-based hospital.

3.3 Enhanced Data Management and Analysis

With **5G's high bandwidth** and **low latency**, healthcare data is transmitted more efficiently, which allows for **better management** and **real-time analysis**.

- **Faster Data Transfer**: High-quality **medical imaging** (e.g., **MRI scans**, **X-rays**, or **CT scans**) can be sent to specialists for analysis in **real-time**, reducing the time it takes to diagnose conditions.
- **AI-Powered Diagnostics**: **5G-enabled telehealth** systems can integrate **artificial intelligence (AI)** to analyze patient data in real time, identifying patterns and predicting future health conditions, such as the early onset of **heart attacks**, **diabetes**, or **stroke**.

4. Challenges of 5G in Telehealth

While the potential of **5G** in **telehealth** is vast, there are also several **challenges** that need to be addressed:

4.1 Data Privacy and Security

As **5G networks** increase the volume of **data transmission** and facilitate the transfer of **sensitive patient data**, **security** and **privacy** become critical concerns. **Data breaches** or **unauthorized access** to healthcare data could lead to severe consequences, including identity theft, financial loss, and harm to patients.

- **Encryption and Secure Communication**: It is essential to encrypt **patient data** during transmission and ensure that all **communications** (video calls, data transfer) are **secure**.

4.2 Cost of Implementation

While **5G** has the potential to reduce healthcare costs in the long term, the initial **implementation costs** of **5G infrastructure**, telehealth **equipment**, and **wearable devices** can be prohibitively high. **Healthcare providers** need to invest in **5G-enabled devices** and **secure data management systems**, which may require significant upfront capital.

4.3 Regulatory and Compliance Issues

The deployment of **telehealth** services must adhere to various **healthcare regulations** and **privacy laws** such as **HIPAA** (in the **U.S.**) or **GDPR** (in **Europe**). Ensuring compliance with these regulations in the context of **5G networks** is a challenge, particularly with the complex nature of **data transmission** and the global reach of **5G**.

The Future of Telehealth with 5G

The integration of **5G technology** in **telehealth** is setting the stage for a **more connected, efficient**, and **accessible healthcare system**. By providing **real-time communication**, **remote monitoring**, and **instant diagnostics**, **5G** enhances **patient care** and makes healthcare services more accessible to people around the world, particularly in underserved regions.

10.3 Healthcare Data Management and Security Challenges

The **healthcare industry** has been undergoing a major digital transformation, driven by advancements in **5G technology**, **electronic health records (EHRs)**, and **telemedicine**. This transformation has made healthcare data collection, sharing, and analysis faster and more efficient, benefiting both healthcare providers and patients. However, it has also raised significant challenges related to **data management** and **security**.

1. The Growing Complexity of Healthcare Data

As **5G networks** continue to expand and more healthcare services move towards **digital platforms**, the volume and complexity of **healthcare data** have increased dramatically. Healthcare data includes **patient records**, **diagnostic imaging**, **biometric data**, **lab test results**, and much more. With the advent of **5G**, this data is being transmitted more frequently, from **wearables** to **surgical robots**, creating an even more intricate network of data flows.

1.1 Types of Healthcare Data

Healthcare data can be categorized into several types, each with its own management and security requirements:

- **Electronic Health Records (EHRs)**: Digital versions of patients' paper charts, containing personal information, medical histories, diagnoses, and treatment plans.
- **Medical Imaging**: Includes **X-rays**, **MRIs**, and **CT scans**, which are high-resolution files requiring significant storage and secure transmission.
- **Patient Monitoring Data**: Includes real-time data collected from devices such as **wearables**, **smartwatches**, or **remote sensors** used for **chronic disease management**.
- **Pharmaceutical Data**: Includes information on medications, dosages, and prescription histories, which need to be updated and accessed regularly.

1.2 Challenges of Managing Healthcare Data

- **Volume and Variety**: Healthcare systems generate vast amounts of data every day. Managing this data requires sophisticated systems capable of handling large volumes and various types of information, from static documents like medical records to dynamic data from **sensors** and **devices**.
- **Interoperability**: Different systems, databases, and devices used by healthcare providers may not be **compatible** with each other, leading to difficulties in sharing and accessing data efficiently across platforms.
- **Real-Time Data Access**: With **5G** enabling continuous patient monitoring, healthcare providers need real-time access to data. However, this access requires fast and secure data storage solutions that can keep pace with the high volume of data being generated.

Practical Example:
In **hospitals**, **patient monitoring systems** are generating data every minute from **wearables**, **ECG machines**, and other connected devices. This data needs to be securely transmitted to **doctors** and **nurses** in real-

time, but the integration of these devices with hospital **EHR systems** can sometimes be complicated. Ensuring **interoperability** between these systems is a key challenge for **data management**.

---

2. Healthcare Data Security: The Risks of 5G Connectivity

The widespread use of **5G technology** in healthcare presents **huge benefits** in terms of **speed** and **efficiency**, but it also introduces new **security risks**. **5G's high speeds** and ability to connect **millions of devices** means that **healthcare data** is constantly in motion, increasing the risk of **data breaches**, **interceptions**, and **cyberattacks**.

2.1 Privacy Risks of Healthcare Data

- **Sensitive Information**: Healthcare data is among the most **sensitive personal information** individuals have. It includes **health records**, **genetic information**, and **personal identifiers**, which must be protected to ensure patient **privacy**.
- **Unauthorized Access**: With more devices connected to the **5G network**, the likelihood of unauthorized access to patient data increases. Hackers could potentially intercept **data streams** or breach hospital **servers** and databases.
- **Data Tracking**: **Location-based services**, enabled by **5G**, can lead to **tracking** patients and healthcare workers. For example, location data from **wearable devices** or **smartphones** could be used to infer sensitive information about a person's **health condition** or **activities**.

2.2 Vulnerabilities in Connected Devices

Healthcare systems are relying more on **Internet of Things (IoT)** devices, such as **patient monitoring sensors**, **wearables**, and **surgical robots**. These devices often communicate data through **5G networks**.

- **Lack of Device Security**: Many **IoT devices** were not designed with **strong security protocols** in mind. Without adequate protection, these devices can serve as entry points for cybercriminals.

- **Data Transmission Risks**: **5G networks** enable faster and more frequent **data transmission**, but this also increases the chances of **data interception** during transmission, especially if **encryption** is not properly implemented.

Practical Example:
In **2020**, a study revealed that over **100,000** IoT devices used in **healthcare** were vulnerable to attacks due to weak or default passwords and inadequate encryption. Attackers could have exploited these vulnerabilities to gain unauthorized access to patient data or even tamper with medical devices.

3. Best Practices for Healthcare Data Management and Security

Given the increasing reliance on **5G** for **data transmission** in healthcare, implementing strong **data management** and **security practices** is essential for protecting patient privacy and ensuring the integrity of healthcare systems. Here are the key practices to follow:

3.1 Data Encryption

Encryption is the first line of defense when it comes to protecting **healthcare data**. Whether it's data in transit (being transmitted between devices or servers) or data at rest (stored on **databases** or **cloud systems**), **encryption** ensures that even if data is intercepted, it remains unreadable.

- **End-to-End Encryption**: Data should be encrypted **end-to-end**, from the point it is collected on a patient's device to the server or healthcare provider's database. This ensures that no unauthorized person can access the data during transmission.

Practical Example:
Verizon Health, a leading **telemedicine provider**, implements **end-to-end encryption** for all **telehealth consultations**. This ensures that the video, audio, and patient data exchanged during virtual consultations are protected from potential cyberattacks or unauthorized access.

3.2 Robust Authentication and Access Control

Strong authentication measures are crucial for protecting sensitive healthcare data. This includes using multi-factor authentication (MFA) for accessing patient records or critical systems. **Role-based access control (RBAC)** should also be implemented to ensure that only authorized healthcare professionals can access specific types of data.

- **MFA for Healthcare Providers**: Healthcare providers should use MFA for accessing **electronic health records (EHRs)** and patient databases. This prevents unauthorized access, even if a password is compromised.
- **Role-Based Access Control**: Only healthcare professionals with the appropriate permissions should be able to access specific patient information. For example, a **nurse** may have access to basic patient data, while a **surgeon** may need access to the patient's full medical history, including surgical notes.

Practical Example:
In **the UK**, the **National Health Service (NHS)** uses **RBAC** in its **EHR system** to ensure that only those with the appropriate credentials (such as **doctors**, **nurses**, or **pharmacists**) can access patient data. This helps protect sensitive information and ensures that only the necessary staff members can view critical health records.

3.3 Real-Time Monitoring and Threat Detection

Healthcare organizations should implement **real-time monitoring** of their **networks** and **devices**. **AI-powered security systems** can analyze traffic patterns and detect anomalies that may signal a potential cyberattack or data breach.

- **Continuous Monitoring**: This involves monitoring all connected devices and **network traffic** for unusual activity. If suspicious behavior is detected—such as a **data breach** or **unauthorized access**—alerts can be sent to security teams to take immediate action.
- **AI and Machine Learning**: **AI and machine learning (ML)** can be used to predict potential security breaches by analyzing large sets of **healthcare data** for anomalies. These technologies help healthcare providers stay ahead of potential attacks by detecting patterns that may otherwise go unnoticed.

Practical Example:
In **Singapore**, **AI-driven security systems** have been implemented in **hospitals** to monitor **real-time data traffic** from **medical devices** and **EHRs**. These systems can quickly detect unusual access patterns, such as multiple failed login attempts or unexpected data transfers, allowing **cybersecurity teams** to respond quickly.

3.4 Compliance with Regulations

Healthcare organizations must comply with **privacy laws** and **regulations** such as **HIPAA (Health Insurance Portability and Accountability Act)** in the U.S., **GDPR (General Data Protection Regulation)** in Europe, and other regional laws that govern **data privacy** and **security**.

- **HIPAA Compliance**: In the U.S., healthcare providers and insurers must comply with **HIPAA**, which mandates **strict guidelines** on the **storage**, **transmission**, and **access** of healthcare data. Failure to comply with HIPAA can result in heavy fines and loss of trust.
- **GDPR Compliance**: For European patients, **GDPR** enforces rules on how patient data is handled, stored, and shared. GDPR also gives patients the **right to access** their personal data and **request corrections** or **deletion** of incorrect or outdated information.

Practical Example:
A **5G-enabled telemedicine platform** operating in Europe must comply with **GDPR**, ensuring that all **healthcare data** transmitted across the network is encrypted, stored securely, and accessible only to authorized users. Additionally, the platform must provide patients with the ability to **opt-out** of data sharing and request **data deletion** if desired.

Overcoming Healthcare Data Management and Security Challenges

As healthcare becomes more **digital**, the need for **strong data management** and **security practices** has never been greater. **5G networks** enable **real-time data** transmission, opening up exciting new possibilities for **remote surgeries**, **patient monitoring**, and **telehealth**.

However, with these advancements come new **security risks** that need to be addressed.

By implementing **end-to-end encryption**, adopting **role-based access control**, utilizing **AI-driven monitoring**, and ensuring **compliance with regulations**, healthcare organizations can build secure systems that protect sensitive patient data while taking full advantage of the **5G-enabled healthcare revolution**.

Chapter 11: 5G in Transportation and Smart Cities

The rapid deployment of **5G technology** is set to revolutionize the way we live, work, and travel. **Transportation** and **smart cities** are two sectors that will benefit immensely from **5G's speed, reliability**, and **low latency**. From **autonomous vehicles** to **smart infrastructure**, **5G** will enable these systems to work more efficiently, safely, and sustainably. In this chapter, we'll explore how **5G** is transforming **transportation** and **smart cities**, and how it's laying the groundwork for a **connected urban future**.

11.1 Autonomous Vehicles and Real-Time Data Exchange

The world of transportation is undergoing a radical transformation with the integration of **autonomous vehicles (AVs)**, also known as **self-driving cars**, and **5G technology**. **5G networks** are enabling **autonomous vehicles** to communicate with each other, infrastructure, and cloud systems in **real-time**, unlocking the potential for safer, more efficient, and sustainable transportation. In this section, we will explore how **5G** supports **autonomous vehicles** and facilitates **real-time data exchange**, which is crucial for enabling these vehicles to operate effectively in a dynamic environment.

1. How 5G Enhances Autonomous Vehicles

1.1 The Role of 5G in Autonomous Vehicles

Autonomous vehicles (AVs) rely on a combination of sensors, cameras, and machine learning algorithms to perceive their surroundings and make driving decisions. These systems need to operate in **real-time** without delays to ensure safe and efficient navigation. This is where **5G's low latency**, **high-speed data transfer**, and **high reliability** come into play.

- **Low Latency**: Autonomous vehicles must react almost instantaneously to their environment. **5G's ultra-low latency** (as low as **1 millisecond**) ensures that data from **sensors**, **radars**, and **cameras** is processed quickly, allowing the vehicle to respond in real-time. In situations like avoiding a pedestrian or making lane changes, even a slight delay in data processing can have significant consequences. **5G's near-instantaneous data transmission** helps eliminate these delays, providing **safety and efficiency**.
- **High-Speed Data Transfer**: Autonomous vehicles generate and process large amounts of data constantly. These include high-definition video feeds, sensor data, and mapping information. **5G's high bandwidth** allows AVs to transmit and receive large data files quickly and efficiently, ensuring smooth operations, whether it's for **vehicle-to-vehicle (V2V)** or **vehicle-to-infrastructure (V2I)** communication.
- **Reliability**: **5G's reliability** is crucial for AVs, especially when they are navigating complex environments or making split-second decisions. A reliable connection ensures that the vehicle can stay connected to the infrastructure around it, such as **traffic signals**, **smart road signs**, and **other vehicles**. This constant exchange of data allows the AV to make informed decisions and optimize its performance in real time.

2. Key Technologies Enabling Real-Time Data Exchange in Autonomous Vehicles

2.1 Vehicle-to-Everything (V2X) Communication

One of the cornerstones of **5G-enabled autonomous vehicles** is **V2X communication**. V2X allows vehicles to communicate with each other (V2V), infrastructure (V2I), and even pedestrians (V2P). This **network of connections** enhances safety, efficiency, and situational awareness by providing real-time data on road conditions, traffic signals, accidents, and more.

- **Vehicle-to-Vehicle (V2V)**: AVs can exchange information with each other, such as **speed**, **location**, and **intentions** (e.g., lane change, turning, braking). By constantly communicating with nearby vehicles, **V2V communication** helps prevent collisions and optimize traffic flow.
- **Vehicle-to-Infrastructure (V2I)**: Vehicles can also communicate with **traffic signals**, **smart signs**, and **road sensors**. For example, an AV can receive a signal from a **traffic light** indicating that it is about to turn red, allowing the vehicle to slow down and avoid unnecessary stops, optimizing fuel efficiency and reducing traffic congestion.
- **Vehicle-to-Pedestrian (V2P)**: **5G-enabled AVs** can also communicate with pedestrians via their **smartphones** or **wearables**, alerting the vehicle when a person is crossing the road, even in situations where the vehicle's sensors might not detect them immediately.

2.2 Real-Time Data Processing and Cloud Integration

Autonomous vehicles rely on **cloud-based systems** to process large amounts of data. These systems use **machine learning algorithms** to analyze data from the vehicle's sensors and make decisions. **5G's high-speed connection** allows **real-time data exchange** between the vehicle and the cloud, ensuring that the AV receives the most up-to-date information for navigation, route planning, and environmental awareness.

- **Real-Time Mapping and Localization**: Autonomous vehicles use **high-definition maps** and **GPS** for navigation. **5G** enables these vehicles to download and update maps in **real-time**, ensuring that they always have the latest information about road conditions, construction zones, and traffic patterns.
- **Cloud-Based AI**: AVs send data to the cloud, where **AI algorithms** analyze it to detect patterns, make predictions, and adjust the vehicle's behavior accordingly. For example, an AV might communicate with the cloud to predict traffic congestion and adjust its route to avoid delays.

3. Benefits of 5G for Autonomous Vehicles

3.1 Safety and Collision Avoidance

The primary goal of **autonomous vehicles** is to improve safety by eliminating human error. **5G** plays a crucial role in achieving this goal by providing real-time data and enabling **instantaneous communication** between vehicles and infrastructure.

- **Collision Avoidance**: With **V2V communication**, AVs can exchange information about their speed, position, and intentions. If two vehicles are on a collision course, **5G-enabled V2V systems** can trigger **automated braking** or **steering adjustments** to avoid accidents.
- **Blind Spot Detection**: 5G allows AVs to **see** beyond their immediate sensors, using data from nearby vehicles or infrastructure. For example, if an AV is about to change lanes, it can receive data from a car in the next lane, alerting the vehicle to any potential blind spot hazards.
- **Predictive Alerts**: AVs can also receive **real-time data** from traffic infrastructure, like upcoming **traffic signals** or **pedestrian crossings**, and adjust their speed or position to enhance safety and reduce the risk of accidents.

Practical Example:
In **Germany**, **5G-enabled autonomous trucks** are being tested in **real-world conditions**. These trucks use **V2V communication** to coordinate lane changes and braking, preventing collisions and enhancing overall safety on highways. The **5G network** provides constant connectivity, enabling the vehicles to exchange **real-time data** with other vehicles and infrastructure.

3.2 Traffic Efficiency and Congestion Reduction

5G-enabled autonomous vehicles can help reduce **traffic congestion** and improve **traffic flow** by communicating with each other and with traffic infrastructure to optimize driving behavior.

- **Optimal Route Selection**: Autonomous vehicles can receive **real-time traffic data** through **V2I communication**, which helps them choose the most efficient routes. For example, if a road is congested, AVs can reroute themselves to avoid delays, improving overall traffic flow.

- **Traffic Light Coordination**: **5G-powered smart traffic lights** can communicate with AVs to adjust **signal timing** based on current traffic conditions. For example, if a line of AVs is approaching an intersection, the system can extend the green light, ensuring smooth passage and reducing wait times.
- **Platoon Driving**: **5G** enables **autonomous vehicles** to travel in **platoons** (groups of vehicles) with minimal space between them. The vehicles in the platoon communicate with each other and adjust their speeds in unison, reducing air drag and improving fuel efficiency.

Practical Example:
In **Singapore, 5G-enabled autonomous buses** are used to improve **public transportation**. These buses communicate with **smart traffic lights** and **other vehicles**, allowing them to optimize routes, reduce delays, and ensure better coordination with other forms of public transit.

3.3 Environmental Impact

5G-enabled autonomous vehicles can have a significant impact on reducing **carbon emissions** and **energy consumption** in the transportation sector.

- **Efficient Driving**: Autonomous vehicles equipped with **5G technology** can drive more smoothly and predictably than human drivers. By optimizing **speed, acceleration**, and **braking**, AVs reduce **fuel consumption** and **emissions**.
- **Eco-Friendly Routing**: By leveraging **real-time traffic data** and **smart infrastructure**, AVs can avoid traffic congestion, reducing idle time and ensuring **efficient travel routes**, which leads to **lower emissions**.

Practical Example:
In **California**, a project called the **Green Autonomous Vehicles Initiative** is exploring how **5G-connected AVs** can improve **fuel efficiency** by optimizing driving behavior and minimizing congestion. The goal is to create a more **sustainable transportation system** while reducing **carbon emissions**.

4. Challenges in Implementing 5G for Autonomous Vehicles

While the potential benefits of **5G in autonomous vehicles** are immense, several challenges remain in making this technology a reality.

4.1 Infrastructure Development

One of the main challenges is the need for extensive **5G infrastructure** to support the data exchange required by AVs. The deployment of **5G networks** in urban and rural areas must be completed before AVs can fully leverage **V2X communication**.

- **5G Network Coverage**: **Autonomous vehicles** require consistent, high-quality **5G coverage** across urban, suburban, and rural areas. This means that **telecom providers** need to install more **5G base stations** and **small cells** in various locations to ensure uninterrupted communication.

4.2 Cybersecurity Risks

The connected nature of **5G-powered autonomous vehicles** makes them vulnerable to **cyberattacks**. Since AVs rely on **real-time data exchange** and **cloud computing**, there is a risk that **malicious actors** could intercept communications, tamper with data, or disrupt vehicle operation.

- **Data Encryption**: **5G networks

** must use **strong encryption** and **security protocols** to protect the data exchanged between vehicles, infrastructure, and the cloud. Additionally, **regular software updates** and **patching** will be essential to protect AVs from evolving security threats.

4.3 Regulatory and Ethical Concerns

As **autonomous vehicles** become more widespread, governments will need to develop new **regulations** for their **operation**, including issues related to liability in the event of accidents, safety standards, and privacy concerns.

- **Ethical Decisions**: Autonomous vehicles will need to be programmed to make difficult ethical decisions in situations where accidents are unavoidable. Developing systems that can make these decisions ethically and transparently will be a significant challenge.

The integration of **5G technology** into **autonomous vehicles** represents a monumental leap forward in the evolution of transportation. With **real-time data exchange**, **low latency**, and **high-speed connectivity**, 5G enables autonomous vehicles to operate more safely, efficiently, and sustainably. While there are challenges related to infrastructure, cybersecurity, and regulation, the potential benefits—ranging from **improved road safety** to **environmental sustainability**—are undeniable.

11.2 Smart Cities: Infrastructure and Efficiency

As urban populations continue to grow, the need for **smarter cities** becomes more pressing. **5G technology** is emerging as a key enabler for creating **smart cities**, providing the infrastructure necessary to support **connected services**, **efficient resource management**, and **improved urban living**. By integrating **5G networks** into the very fabric of city infrastructure, cities can become more **efficient**, **sustainable**, and **livable**.

1. What Makes a City "Smart"?

A **smart city** leverages **information technology** and **data** to optimize the performance of city services and infrastructure. This involves integrating **sensors**, **actuators**, and **data networks** to collect, analyze, and act on real-time information. In a smart city, everything—from **traffic management** to **waste collection**—is interconnected and optimized for efficiency and sustainability.

Key characteristics of a **smart city** include:

- **Connected Infrastructure**: Cities integrate **smart grids**, **intelligent streetlights**, **public transport systems**, and **sensor networks** for real-time monitoring and decision-making.
- **Data-Driven Decision Making**: Cities use real-time data to optimize resources and improve services, from managing energy consumption to enhancing public safety.
- **Sustainability**: Smart cities aim to reduce **environmental impact**, increase **energy efficiency**, and improve **quality of life** for citizens through innovative technologies.

Why 5G is Essential for Smart Cities

5G provides the **high-speed** connectivity and **low latency** necessary for smart cities to function at their best. It enables **real-time data transmission** and **cloud-based decision-making**, ensuring the city's systems can respond to changing conditions instantaneously.

---

2. 5G-Driven Infrastructure for Smart Cities

2.1 Smart Grid and Energy Management

A **smart grid** is an essential part of any **smart city**. It uses digital technology to monitor and manage the flow of **electricity** from **generation points** to **consumers**, allowing for more efficient and reliable energy use.

- **5G-enabled Smart Meters**: With **5G**, smart meters can communicate energy usage data in real-time. These **smart meters** can send data to **energy providers** and **grid operators** instantly, allowing for dynamic pricing, immediate response to demand fluctuations, and optimized energy distribution.
- **Demand Response**: With **real-time data** from the **smart grid**, energy providers can adjust the supply of electricity based on demand. This ensures **energy efficiency**, reduces costs, and minimizes waste.
- **Renewable Energy Integration**: **5G networks** allow for better integration of **renewable energy sources** like **solar panels** and **wind turbines**. Smart grids can adjust in real-time to fluctuations

in energy production from renewable sources, ensuring that electricity supply meets demand without relying on fossil fuels.

Practical Example:
In **New York City**, the **Con Edison** smart grid project integrates **real-time data** from **5G-connected smart meters** and **grid sensors** to monitor and optimize energy usage. This system helps reduce **energy waste**, lower **operational costs**, and allow **residents** to monitor and manage their **electricity consumption** more effectively.

2.2 Intelligent Transportation Systems (ITS)

Transportation is one of the most critical aspects of urban infrastructure. **5G technology** enables **smart transportation systems** that improve traffic management, enhance the efficiency of public transit, and reduce congestion.

- **Real-Time Traffic Management**: With **5G-enabled sensors** embedded in roads, traffic signals, and vehicles, cities can collect and transmit traffic data in real-time. This data can then be analyzed to optimize traffic flow, reduce congestion, and improve travel times.
- **Autonomous Vehicles**: **5G** enables autonomous vehicles to communicate with each other and with city infrastructure. This communication helps autonomous vehicles avoid collisions, adjust speed, and share information about road conditions, ensuring **smooth traffic flow** and **reduced accidents**.
- **Smart Public Transportation**: With **5G powered public transit**, cities can track the real-time locations of buses, trains, and other forms of public transportation. **Smart buses** can communicate with **traffic lights** to adjust their routes or avoid delays, optimizing the **entire transport network**.

Practical Example:
London has implemented a **smart traffic management system** that uses **5G technology** to control **traffic lights** dynamically based on real-time traffic conditions. This system not only improves **traffic flow** but also reduces **fuel consumption** by minimizing **idling time** at traffic signals.

3. Efficiency and Sustainability in Smart Cities

3.1 Waste Management and Smart Bins

Waste management in cities is a growing challenge, especially with **increasing urban populations**. **5G technology** can significantly improve the efficiency of waste collection and recycling processes.

- **Smart Bins**: **5G-enabled bins** equipped with sensors can detect when they are full and notify waste management teams. This reduces unnecessary trips and ensures that waste is collected on time, reducing congestion in waste collection routes.
- **Optimized Waste Collection**: With real-time data from **smart bins**, waste collection routes can be dynamically adjusted to focus on areas with higher volumes of waste. This not only reduces fuel consumption but also ensures that waste is picked up on time, keeping cities cleaner and reducing landfill waste.

Practical Example:
In **Barcelona**, the city has implemented a **smart waste collection system** using **5G-connected sensors** placed in **waste bins**. These sensors detect when bins are full, automatically notifying the waste collection team. This system has reduced **unnecessary trips**, optimized waste collection, and improved the overall efficiency of **municipal waste management**.

3.2 Water Management and Leak Detection

Water management is a critical component of urban sustainability. **5G technology** enables real-time monitoring of water systems, improving efficiency and reducing waste.

- **Smart Water Meters**: With **5G-enabled smart meters**, water usage data is collected and transmitted in real time. This enables **utilities** to detect leaks, track consumption patterns, and offer more accurate billing to consumers.
- **Leak Detection**: **5G sensors** embedded in water pipes can detect leaks in real-time, allowing authorities to quickly fix issues before they cause major damage or waste significant amounts of water.
- **Sustainable Water Use**: **Real-time monitoring** of water distribution helps cities optimize water usage, ensuring that it is

distributed efficiently, reducing waste, and ensuring that scarce water resources are used sustainably.

Practical Example:
In **Amsterdam**, the city has implemented **5G-powered smart water management systems** to detect leaks and optimize water distribution. Sensors embedded in **water pipes** send real-time data to a **centralized control system**, allowing for quicker leak detection and a more efficient water distribution system.

---

4. Enhancing Public Safety with 5G

Public safety is an essential aspect of **smart cities**, and **5G technology** plays a significant role in improving **surveillance**, **emergency response**, and **crime prevention**.

4.1 Real-Time Surveillance and Incident Response

- **Smart Cameras**: **5G-connected cameras** placed in key urban areas can provide real-time, high-quality video feeds to law enforcement and emergency services. These cameras can **identify criminal activity** or **track suspicious behavior**, enabling a faster response time.
- **Crowd Management**: During large public events, **5G-enabled sensors** can monitor crowd density and movement in real-time. This data can be analyzed to prevent overcrowding, alert authorities to potential risks, and ensure public safety.

Practical Example:
In **Chicago**, **5G-powered surveillance cameras** have been integrated into the city's **public safety systems**. The cameras can transmit **high-definition video** to local police stations in real-time, enabling officers to assess the situation and respond quickly, improving **public safety** in high-risk areas.

4.2 Emergency Services and First Responders

- **Real-Time Communication**: **5G technology** allows **ambulances**, **fire trucks**, and **police vehicles** to communicate in real-time with city infrastructure and control centers, optimizing their routes and ensuring that emergency services can reach their destinations as quickly as possible.

- **AI and Predictive Analytics**: In a **smart city**, data from emergency services and other sources can be analyzed using **AI** to predict where incidents are likely to occur. This helps allocate resources efficiently and reduces response times.

Practical Example:
In **Los Angeles**, **5G-enabled smart traffic management** systems communicate with **ambulance** and **fire truck fleets**, optimizing routes and reducing response times. This system ensures that emergency services can bypass traffic congestion and reach their destinations more quickly.

---

5. The Future of 5G in Smart Cities

As **5G networks** continue to expand, cities around the world are embracing **5G-powered solutions** to enhance infrastructure, improve efficiency, and promote sustainability. Over the next decade, **5G-enabled smart cities** will become more **integrated**, **autonomous**, and **efficient**.

- **Urban Mobility**: With **5G**, we can expect **autonomous vehicles**, **smart public transport**, and **integrated traffic management** systems that are more efficient, safer, and environmentally friendly.
- **Sustainability**: By optimizing energy use, water management, waste collection, and public services, **5G** will play a crucial role in making cities more **sustainable** and **resilient** to environmental challenges.
- **Citizen-Centric Services**: With **5G**, cities will be able to offer more **personalized** services, from **healthcare** and **education** to **energy** and **transportation**, making life easier for residents and improving **quality of life**.

5G technology is at the heart of the next generation of **smart cities**, where **connected infrastructure** meets **data-driven decision-making** to create **efficient**, **sustainable**, and **livable urban environments**. From **energy**

optimization and **smart traffic systems** to **public safety** and **environmental management**, **5G** is enabling cities to address their most pressing challenges while improving the quality of life for their residents.

11.3 Traffic Management, Safety, and Environmental Impact

As cities around the world continue to grow, the complexity of managing urban transportation systems escalates. **Traffic congestion**, **accidents**, and **environmental pollution** are persistent challenges that require smart solutions. **5G technology**, with its **high-speed connectivity** and **low-latency communication**, has the potential to address these issues by transforming the way cities manage **traffic flow**, **ensure safety**, and reduce their **environmental footprint**.

1. Traffic Management: Optimizing Flow with Real-Time Data

5G networks are fundamentally changing how cities manage traffic. By enabling the **real-time collection** and **processing** of traffic data, cities can now make smarter decisions that optimize **traffic flow**, reduce congestion, and minimize delays.

1.1 Real-Time Traffic Monitoring and Control

With **5G-enabled sensors** embedded in roadways, **traffic lights**, and vehicles, cities can monitor traffic in real-time, adjusting signals and flow based on current conditions.

- **Smart Traffic Lights**: Traditional traffic lights work on fixed schedules or preset timers. With **5G**, **traffic lights** can be connected to a **centralized system** that collects data from **sensors** and **cameras** across the city. This system can then adjust signal timing based on factors like **real-time traffic flow**, **accidents**, or **special events**.

- **Dynamic Traffic Routing**: **5G-powered systems** can analyze real-time data to suggest alternate routes for drivers based on **congestion** or **road closures**. In case of an **accident** or **construction zone**, the system can quickly re-route traffic, ensuring minimal delays for travelers.
- **Vehicle-to-Infrastructure (V2I) Communication**: **5G** enables vehicles to communicate with **traffic lights** and **smart road signs**. For instance, if a vehicle approaches an intersection, **5G communication** allows the car to receive real-time information about the traffic light's status, allowing it to adjust its speed to avoid unnecessary stops, thereby reducing fuel consumption and emissions.

Practical Example:
In **Chicago**, the city is testing a **5G-enabled traffic management system** that uses **smart traffic signals**. These signals adjust the timing of lights based on real-time data from **cameras** and **sensors** placed at intersections. The system has helped reduce **waiting times**, **cut congestion**, and improved overall **traffic flow** in key areas.

1.2 Predictive Traffic Management

With **5G's low latency** and high-speed data transmission, cities can use **predictive analytics** to manage traffic proactively rather than reactively. By analyzing data from various sources, such as **smart cameras**, **road sensors**, and **social media**, traffic management systems can forecast potential congestion points and prepare solutions before traffic bottlenecks occur.

- **Traffic Prediction**: Using **real-time data** on traffic patterns, **weather conditions**, and **events**, predictive systems can anticipate traffic jams and suggest alternative routes or adjust signal timings preemptively.
- **Event-Based Traffic Management**: Large-scale events like **concerts**, **sports games**, or **conferences** generate massive traffic surges. **5G networks** can process data from event schedules and crowd movements to prepare the traffic system in advance, directing more vehicles toward available routes and reducing congestion.

Practical Example:
In **Seoul**, a **5G-powered predictive traffic management system** has been introduced. The system analyzes **real-time traffic data** and **weather conditions** to forecast traffic congestion during the morning and evening rush hours. By using this information, the system can adjust **traffic signals** dynamically and suggest alternate routes to drivers, minimizing congestion and improving traffic flow.

2. Traffic Safety: Enhancing Security and Reducing Accidents

The ultimate goal of any traffic management system is to make the roads safer for everyone. **5G technology** plays a pivotal role in improving traffic **safety** by providing instant communication between vehicles, pedestrians, and infrastructure, ensuring quick responses to potential hazards.

2.1 Vehicle-to-Vehicle (V2V) and Vehicle-to-Pedestrian (V2P) Communication

One of the most promising features of **5G** in **traffic safety** is **vehicle-to-vehicle (V2V)** and **vehicle-to-pedestrian (V2P)** communication. These systems allow cars to communicate directly with each other and with pedestrians, providing an extra layer of safety.

- **V2V Communication**: **Autonomous and connected vehicles** can share real time data on their speed, location, and direction. If two cars are on a collision course, **5G-powered V2V communication** allows them to instantly alert each other, triggering safety measures like **automatic braking** or **steering adjustments** to avoid an accident.
- **V2P Communication**: **Pedestrians** with **smartphones** or **wearables** can send signals to nearby vehicles, alerting them to their presence at a crosswalk or intersection. This can prevent accidents, particularly in poorly lit or high-traffic areas.

Practical Example:
In **Sweden**, a **5G-based V2V and V2P system** is being tested in which **autonomous cars** communicate with **pedestrians** wearing **smart devices**. When a pedestrian steps onto the crosswalk, the car receives a real-time

notification and adjusts its speed or stops, ensuring safety for both the pedestrian and the driver.

2.2 Smart Surveillance and Incident Detection

5G-powered smart surveillance systems use **cameras** and **sensors** placed in critical areas of the city to monitor traffic and detect incidents such as **accidents, pedestrian crossings**, or **dangerous driving behavior**.

- **Real-Time Incident Alerts**: When an **incident** is detected, the system can instantly send data to **emergency responders**, who can then reach the scene more quickly. The system can also trigger **traffic lights** to clear the way for emergency vehicles, reducing response times.
- **Smart Cameras**: **5G cameras** placed in high-traffic areas or problem zones can analyze footage in real time, detecting accidents or unsafe driving behavior. If dangerous conditions are detected, the system can send alerts to nearby vehicles, advising them to slow down or take alternative routes.

Practical Example:
In **Singapore**, **5G-enabled smart cameras** have been deployed to monitor intersections and busy roads. These cameras can detect accidents, abnormal traffic patterns, or pedestrian activity, alerting **emergency services** and **drivers** to potential hazards. This proactive system has significantly reduced **response times** and **accidents** in high-traffic areas.

3. Environmental Impact: Reducing Carbon Footprint and Improving Sustainability

One of the most significant challenges of modern transportation is its impact on the environment. Cities are grappling with **traffic congestion**, **air pollution**, and **greenhouse gas emissions** caused by **inefficient transportation systems**. **5G technology** can play a key role in reducing the environmental impact of urban mobility.

3.1 Eco-Friendly Traffic Flow Management

5G-enabled traffic management systems help reduce fuel consumption and **emissions** by optimizing traffic flow and reducing congestion.

- **Reducing Idling Time**: **5G** can help minimize **idling time** at traffic signals. By enabling **smart traffic signals** that adjust based on real-time traffic data, **5G** helps vehicles move smoothly, avoiding unnecessary stops and starts, which leads to **lower fuel consumption** and **reduced emissions**.
- **Green Traffic Routes**: By integrating **real-time data** from traffic sensors, **5G systems** can prioritize **green traffic routes**, allowing vehicles to pass through intersections with minimal delay and reduce carbon emissions from idling.

Practical Example:
In **London**, a **5G-powered smart traffic management system** has been deployed to prioritize **public transport** and **low-emission vehicles**. This system helps reduce the carbon footprint by ensuring that **green buses** and **electric vehicles** can pass through intersections with minimal delays, encouraging the use of more sustainable modes of transportation.

3.2 Smart Parking Systems and Reduced Circling

Another significant contributor to **urban pollution** is the time spent searching for parking. **5G-enabled smart parking systems** can help reduce the **carbon footprint** of cities by efficiently managing parking resources.

- **Real-Time Parking Data**: **5G sensors** embedded in parking spaces can provide real-time information on parking availability. Drivers can be guided to the nearest available spot without wasting time driving around looking for parking, which reduces fuel consumption and congestion.
- **Dynamic Parking Pricing**: **5G networks** can also enable dynamic pricing for parking. Prices can increase in high-demand areas and decrease in less busy parts of the city, encouraging drivers to park in areas with less congestion and reducing the overall carbon footprint.

Practical Example:
In **San Francisco**, a **5G-connected smart parking system** has been implemented to guide drivers to available parking spots using real-time

data. This system has helped reduce **search time** by up to **30%**, minimizing fuel consumption and lowering **CO_2 emissions**.

5G technology is transforming the way cities manage **traffic**, ensuring **safer**, **more efficient**, and **environmentally sustainable** transportation systems. Through **real-time data exchange**, **vehicle-to-vehicle** and **vehicle-to-infrastructure communication**, and **smart traffic management**, 5G is enabling cities to tackle congestion, improve safety, and reduce their carbon footprint.

By integrating **5G** into **traffic management** systems, **public transportation**, and **environmental monitoring**, cities can create more **livable** and **sustainable** urban environments. The potential benefits of **5G** in transportation and urban mobility are immense, and as **5G networks** continue to expand, we will see more cities adopting **smart solutions** to address the transportation challenges of the 21st century.

Chapter 12: 5G in Manufacturing and Industry 4.0

The rise of **5G technology** is one of the most transformative factors in the ongoing evolution of **manufacturing**, giving birth to what is commonly known as **Industry 4.0**. This new industrial revolution leverages **advanced technologies** such as **artificial intelligence (AI)**, **robotics**, and **real-time data analytics** to drive **efficiency, automation**, and **sustainability** in manufacturing processes. As **5G networks** expand globally, their ability to provide **high-speed connectivity, low latency**, and **reliable communication** between machines, devices, and systems will enable the **manufacturing industry** to operate smarter and more efficiently.

12.1 Robotics and Automation in Manufacturing

The manufacturing industry has been undergoing a dramatic transformation, and at the heart of this shift is **robotics** and **automation**. Coupled with the power of **5G technology**, the potential for improving production efficiency, precision, and safety in manufacturing has reached new heights. In this section, we will explore how **5G** enhances **robotics and automation**, providing insights into their applications in the manufacturing sector.

1. The Role of Robotics and Automation in Manufacturing

Robotics and automation refer to the use of machines or computer-controlled systems to carry out tasks traditionally performed by humans. In manufacturing, this can include everything from assembling parts to packaging products. Robotics allows manufacturers to achieve higher **productivity**, **precision**, and **speed** while reducing human error and safety risks.

1.1 The Evolution of Robotics in Manufacturing

- **Early Robotics**: Early robotic systems in manufacturing were often limited to simple, repetitive tasks such as **welding** and **painting** in automotive production lines. These robots worked in isolated environments, disconnected from the rest of the factory's equipment.
- **Modern Robotics**: Today's robotics are more sophisticated. They are **connected**, **autonomous**, and capable of performing a wide range of tasks with **high precision**. These modern systems are integrated into the larger **Industry 4.0 ecosystem**, where data from sensors, machines, and robots is shared in real-time to enable dynamic decision-making.

5G Technology plays a critical role in these advancements by enabling faster communication, higher data throughput, and the ability to support a network of connected devices in manufacturing environments.

2. How 5G Enhances Robotics and Automation

2.1 Low Latency for Real-Time Operation

Latency refers to the delay between sending a signal and receiving a response. In robotics, low latency is crucial for operations that require precision and real-time decision-making.

- **5G's Ultra-Low Latency**: One of the key advantages of **5G networks** is their **low latency** (as low as **1 millisecond**), which allows robots to perform tasks without noticeable delays. For instance, in a **production line** where multiple robotic arms must work together, any delay in communication between these arms could cause bottlenecks or errors in assembly. **5G's near-instantaneous data transmission** ensures smooth coordination among robots, optimizing workflow.
- **Real-Time Feedback and Adjustments**: Robots can adjust their actions in real-time based on sensor data, such as the **position of parts** or **robot orientation**. With **5G**, the data from these sensors is transmitted without delays, allowing robots to correct

themselves as they work, ensuring precision and minimizing defects.

Practical Example:
In **Tesla's Gigafactory**, **5G-enabled robotic systems** are used to assemble electric vehicles. The robots can communicate in real-time with other machines on the assembly line, adjusting their actions based on live feedback. This high level of coordination reduces production time and ensures the quality of every vehicle.

2.2 High-Speed Data Transfer for Enhanced Precision

Modern robots rely heavily on **data transfer** to function effectively. Whether it's **computer vision systems** for object recognition or **force sensors** for picking and placing items, **high-speed data transfer** is essential for their operation.

- **5G's High Bandwidth**: **5G networks** offer **higher data transfer speeds** than previous generations of wireless networks. This means that robots can process more complex datasets faster and act on that information immediately. For instance, a robot using **3D vision systems** to pick up fragile components will require a constant flow of high-quality image data, which can be transmitted almost instantly via **5G**.
- **Real-Time Remote Control and Monitoring**: Manufacturers can also take advantage of **5G's high-speed connectivity** to remotely control or monitor robots in real-time. This is especially useful in environments that are dangerous for humans, such as in hazardous material handling or high-temperature environments.

Practical Example:
ABB Robotics, a leader in industrial robotics, has developed **5G-enabled robotic arms** that utilize **high-definition cameras** and **real-time data processing** for precision assembly tasks. These robots are part of **automated production lines** where high-speed communication ensures smooth operation and high-quality results.

3. Collaborative Robots (Cobots)

One of the most exciting developments in **robotics** is the advent of **collaborative robots** (or **cobots**). Unlike traditional robots that work independently from humans, **cobots** are designed to work alongside human operators, sharing tasks and adjusting their actions based on human input.

3.1 Enhancing Collaboration with 5G

- **5G and Cobots**: **5G networks** allow **cobots** to communicate more effectively with human workers. These robots can react to human gestures, instructions, or even safety concerns in real-time. For example, if a human worker approaches a **robotic arm**, the cobot can slow down or stop to prevent injury.
- **Real-Time Interaction**: **5G's low latency** enables seamless interaction between robots and humans, even in complex and fast-paced manufacturing environments. With **5G-powered cobots**, the speed of collaboration can increase, allowing for flexible and adaptive manufacturing processes.
- **Task Sharing**: In many cases, cobots are designed to perform tasks that complement human capabilities. For example, a **robotic arm** can lift heavy parts, while a human worker can focus on **assembly** or **quality control**. **5G technology** ensures that both the robot and the human can operate in harmony, without delays or miscommunication.

Practical Example:
In **Universal Robots'** product line, **cobots** are used to assist with a variety of tasks, from **assembly** to **testing**. With the integration of **5G**, these robots are able to adjust their movements based on human input and even communicate with other machines in real-time. In a car manufacturing plant, for example, the cobot may hand a part to a human operator, who then places it onto a conveyor belt. The interaction between human and machine is seamless, thanks to **5G-enabled collaboration**.

4. The Impact of 5G on Manufacturing Operations

4.1 Increased Efficiency and Reduced Downtime

Manufacturers are under constant pressure to produce high-quality products at lower costs and faster speeds. By integrating **5G-powered robots** into their operations, manufacturers can achieve **higher efficiency** and **reduce downtime**.

- **Predictive Maintenance**: **5G-enabled robots** can continuously monitor their own performance and **predict when maintenance is needed**. For example, a robot can send data about its **motors, hydraulic systems**, or **motion sensors** to a centralized system. Based on this data, maintenance teams can schedule repairs or replacements before a failure occurs, preventing costly downtime.
- **Automation of Routine Tasks**: Robots can take over repetitive and time-consuming tasks, such as **part picking, welding**, or **packaging**, allowing human workers to focus on more complex or creative tasks. With **5G**, robots can communicate with **other machines** or **centralized systems** to synchronize their operations, reducing wait times and improving overall productivity.

Practical Example:
In **Volkswagen's smart factory**, **5G-enabled robots** work in unison to perform routine tasks such as **welding** and **part assembly**. Using **predictive maintenance** tools, robots can report their status to a central monitoring system, which triggers maintenance if needed. This system has helped **Volkswagen** reduce production delays by ensuring that robots are always performing optimally.

4.2 Flexibility and Scalability

Another key benefit of integrating **5G-powered robots** into manufacturing is their **flexibility** and **scalability**. **5G's high bandwidth** allows robots to perform tasks that require **dynamic adjustments** based on real-time data. Additionally, robots can be quickly reprogrammed or moved between different parts of the factory to handle changing production needs.

- **Rapid Reconfiguration**: If a manufacturer needs to switch from producing one product to another, **5G-enabled robots** can be quickly **reprogrammed** or even **moved** to different areas of the factory to accommodate the change in production.
- **Scalability**: As production demands increase, manufacturers can deploy more robots with minimal disruption. Since **5G networks**

can handle **high-density device connectivity**, manufacturers can scale their robotic operations without worrying about network congestion or performance degradation.

Practical Example:
At **Siemens' Amberg** facility, **robots** are used for **product assembly** across a variety of product lines. As demand for different products changes, the **5G-enabled robots** can be easily **reprogrammed** or relocated to new stations, ensuring continuous production and minimal downtime. This flexibility allows Siemens to adapt to market needs quickly, keeping production costs low and lead times short.

5. The Future of Robotics in Manufacturing with 5G

The future of **robotics** and **automation** in manufacturing is bright, particularly with the expansion of **5G networks**. As more industries embrace **Industry 4.0**, the integration of **5G-enabled robotics** will lead to even smarter, more autonomous manufacturing systems.

5.1 Full Automation and Integration

In the future, **full automation** driven by **5G networks** could enable entire factories to run autonomously. **Robots** and **AI systems** could collaborate seamlessly to manage everything from **production lines** to **inventory control**.

5.2 AI-Powered Robotics

The integration of **artificial intelligence** (AI) with **5G-powered robots

** will allow these machines to make **intelligent decisions** based on real-time data. AI will enable robots to learn from their environment, adapt to changing conditions, and improve their performance over time.

5.3 Collaborative, Autonomous Workforces

As **cobots** continue to evolve, robots will work alongside humans more efficiently, creating **hybrid workforces** that combine human creativity with machine precision. **5G networks** will allow these **collaborative

robots to communicate, learn, and evolve in real time, further enhancing the **flexibility** and **efficiency** of manufacturing operations.

The integration of **5G technology** into **robotics** and **automation** is driving the next wave of **manufacturing innovation**. From **real-time communication** and **precision** to **predictive maintenance** and **collaborative robots**, 5G is enabling **smarter**, **faster**, and **more flexible** manufacturing operations. With **5G**, manufacturers are equipped to meet the demands of an increasingly competitive, dynamic, and complex industry landscape.

12.2 Real-Time Monitoring and Predictive Maintenance

In the rapidly evolving world of **manufacturing**, staying ahead of equipment failures and maintaining optimal performance is crucial for maximizing productivity and minimizing downtime. This is where **real-time monitoring** and **predictive maintenance** come into play. **5G technology** is set to revolutionize these areas, enabling manufacturers to monitor their machinery and processes in real time and predict when maintenance is required before costly failures occur. This chapter will explore how **5G-powered real-time monitoring** and **predictive maintenance** are reshaping the manufacturing landscape, providing tangible benefits in terms of efficiency, cost reduction, and improved reliability.

1. Real-Time Monitoring: The Backbone of Modern Manufacturing

Real-time monitoring refers to the continuous collection and analysis of data from machines, sensors, and devices as they operate. This data can include everything from temperature and vibration levels to operational efficiency and output quality. With the introduction of **5G networks**, this process has become faster, more reliable, and more scalable, empowering manufacturers to make data-driven decisions that enhance performance.

1.1 How 5G Enhances Real-Time Monitoring

- **High-Speed Data Transfer**: One of the defining features of **5G** is its ability to transfer data at **much higher speeds** than previous network technologies, such as **4G**. In a manufacturing setting, this allows real-time data from **IoT sensors**, **smart machines**, and **robots** to be sent to centralized systems without delays, ensuring immediate insights into equipment performance.
- **Low Latency Communication**: 5G's **ultra-low latency** (as low as **1 millisecond**) enables instantaneous communication between machines and control systems. This is critical in industries that rely on fast responses, such as **automotive** and **electronics manufacturing**, where real-time adjustments to production processes can prevent errors, defects, and material waste.
- **Massive Device Connectivity**: **5G networks** can support the simultaneous connection of **millions of devices** within a factory. Whether it's **sensors**, **cameras**, or other smart devices, **5G** ensures that each device communicates seamlessly with others, providing a unified view of the entire operation. This is vital for industries that use **large-scale automation** or **distributed networks** of machines.

Practical Example:
In **Siemens' Amberg Electronics Plant** in Germany, **5G-enabled smart sensors** are embedded throughout the factory to collect real-time data on **machine performance**, **temperature**, **vibration levels**, and more. This data is transmitted via **5G networks** to a centralized system, allowing operators to monitor equipment health and make immediate adjustments as needed.

1.2 Benefits of Real-Time Monitoring

- **Improved Efficiency**: By monitoring machine health in real time, manufacturers can detect issues as soon as they arise. For example, if a motor is running too hot, sensors can trigger an alert, prompting maintenance before the machine fails. This reduces unplanned downtime and helps maintain a smooth production flow.

- **Quality Control**: **5G-powered monitoring systems** allow operators to track the quality of each item as it moves along the production line. Using **real-time data** from cameras or **machine vision systems**, they can detect defects, misalignments, or other issues immediately and take corrective action before faulty products are sent out.
- **Resource Optimization**: **Real-time monitoring** also enables more efficient use of resources. Manufacturers can track energy consumption, materials usage, and machine load, optimizing processes to reduce waste and energy costs.

2. Predictive Maintenance: Avoiding Downtime Before It Happens

Predictive maintenance is an advanced maintenance strategy that uses data and algorithms to predict when a machine is likely to fail, allowing for maintenance to be scheduled before a breakdown occurs. Unlike traditional methods that rely on **time-based schedules** or **reactive repairs**, **predictive maintenance** leverages **real-time data** to improve accuracy, reduce downtime, and save costs.

2.1 How 5G Enables Predictive Maintenance

- **Continuous Data Collection**: **5G technology** supports the continuous collection of data from **IoT sensors** placed on machinery. These sensors monitor variables such as **temperature, vibration, pressure**, and **rotation speed**. As machines operate, the data is transmitted in real-time to a central system for analysis. **5G's low latency** allows for almost immediate processing and feedback, enabling early detection of potential issues.
- **Data Analysis and Machine Learning**: The real power of **predictive maintenance** comes from the **data analytics** and **machine learning (ML) algorithms** that analyze the incoming data to identify patterns. For example, if a machine's vibration levels consistently exceed normal thresholds, predictive algorithms can recognize this as a precursor to failure and trigger maintenance before the problem becomes severe.
- **Edge Computing**: In some cases, **5G networks** enable **edge computing**, where data is processed close to the source (i.e., on the

machine itself or a nearby gateway). This reduces the time it takes to identify and act on issues, especially in critical manufacturing environments where split-second decisions are necessary.

Practical Example:
General Electric (GE) uses **5G-enabled IoT sensors** to monitor **turbines** in **wind farms**. These sensors collect real-time data on factors like **vibration** and **temperature**. The data is processed via **edge computing** systems, which can detect potential issues and notify technicians to perform maintenance before a failure occurs, preventing costly downtime and maximizing the lifespan of the turbines.

2.2 Benefits of Predictive Maintenance

- **Reduced Downtime**: The most obvious benefit of **predictive maintenance** is the reduction in **unplanned downtime**. By addressing issues before they cause machine failure, manufacturers can avoid the costly delays that come with emergency repairs and production stoppages.
- **Cost Savings**: **Predictive maintenance** helps manufacturers avoid the cost of **over-maintaining** equipment. Instead of performing routine maintenance on every machine at fixed intervals, maintenance activities are performed only when necessary. This leads to a significant reduction in maintenance costs and extends the life of equipment.
- **Improved Safety**: By predicting and preventing equipment failures, **predictive maintenance** improves workplace safety. For instance, preventing a motor failure in a high-risk environment can avoid potential accidents or hazardous situations for workers.

3. Real-Time Monitoring and Predictive Maintenance in Action: Practical Implementation

To bring these concepts to life, let's walk through a step-by-step example of how **5G-powered real-time monitoring** and **predictive maintenance** could be applied in a **factory** setting.

Step 1: Installing IoT Sensors and Devices

The first step is to install **IoT sensors** on critical machinery and equipment throughout the manufacturing facility. These sensors could measure variables such as temperature, vibration, pressure, and motor speed. For example, **smart vibration sensors** can be placed on motors and pumps, and **temperature sensors** can be placed on furnaces and ovens.

Step 2: Connecting Sensors to 5G Network

Next, these sensors are connected to the **5G network**. Thanks to **5G's high bandwidth and low latency**, data from thousands of sensors can be sent simultaneously to a **centralized data platform** without overwhelming the network. This allows for seamless communication and the ability to monitor machines in real-time.

Step 3: Data Transmission and Analysis

The data is continuously transmitted and processed by advanced **data analytics platforms**. **Machine learning algorithms** analyze the incoming data to detect patterns or anomalies that indicate a potential failure. For example, if a machine's temperature rises beyond the normal operating range, the system will flag this as a potential issue.

Step 4: Predictive Maintenance Triggers

Once a potential issue is identified, **predictive maintenance algorithms** predict when the failure is likely to occur. The system might recommend specific maintenance actions, such as lubricating a part or replacing a worn-out component. Based on this prediction, the system schedules maintenance during off-peak hours, avoiding disruption to production.

Step 5: Notification and Action

Finally, the system sends a **real-time alert** to maintenance personnel, who can take the appropriate action. The **5G network** enables technicians to receive notifications and access detailed diagnostics through **mobile apps** or **AR glasses**, providing them with the information they need to fix the problem quickly.

Practical Example:
Rolls-Royce has implemented a **5G-based predictive maintenance system** on its **aerospace engines**. The company's engines are fitted with

IoT sensors that collect real-time data on variables like **vibration** and **temperature**. Using **5G**, this data is sent to **cloud-based analytics platforms** where machine learning algorithms predict when an engine might need maintenance. The predictive system alerts Rolls-Royce technicians, who can then perform maintenance before a failure occurs, improving engine reliability and reducing downtime.

4. Challenges and Considerations

While **5G-powered real-time monitoring** and **predictive maintenance** offer immense benefits, there are some challenges that manufacturers need to address:

4.1 Data Security and Privacy

Since real-time monitoring and predictive maintenance involve the constant exchange of sensitive data, manufacturers must ensure that their **5G networks** are secure. This includes encrypting **data in transit** and ensuring that only authorized personnel can access critical machine data.

4.2 Integration with Legacy Systems

Many factories still use legacy equipment that may not be compatible with modern **IoT sensors** or **5G networks**. Upgrading these systems can be expensive and time-consuming, so it's important for manufacturers to find ways to integrate **new technologies** with their existing systems without disrupting production.

4.3 Scalability and Maintenance

As manufacturers scale their operations, they must ensure that their **5G networks** can handle the increasing number of connected devices and sensors. Additionally, the predictive maintenance system itself requires ongoing **maintenance** and fine-tuning to ensure that it remains accurate as the system grows.

The integration of **5G-powered real-time monitoring** and **predictive maintenance** in manufacturing is transforming the industry, allowing for smarter, more efficient operations. By continuously collecting and analyzing data from machines and sensors, manufacturers can predict and prevent equipment failures, reducing downtime, cutting costs, and improving overall productivity. As **5G networks** continue to roll out globally, the ability to monitor and maintain complex systems in real time will become a standard practice in the manufacturing world, making operations more reliable, cost-effective, and efficient than ever before.

Part 5: The Future of 5G and Beyond

Chapter 13: Beyond 5G: What Comes Next?

The rollout of **5G** networks has sparked a revolution across industries—from **healthcare** and **transportation** to **manufacturing** and **entertainment**. But as we begin to experience the transformative effects of **5G**, we're already asking: What comes next? The road beyond 5G is paved with promises of even faster, more reliable technologies, and a vision of a world that's more **connected** and **intelligent** than ever before. In this chapter, we'll explore the exciting future of **6G**, how **5G** is laying the foundation for **AI** and the **Internet of Things (IoT)**, and the **global impact** of these technologies in shaping economies and digital societies.

13.1 The Road to 6G and Future Technologies

The **journey to 6G** is not just an incremental step from **5G**, but rather a leap forward into a **hyperconnected** world where **speed**, **intelligence**, and **automation** converge. As **5G** continues to transform industries, there's already a growing focus on the next phase of mobile technology—**6G**. The goal of **6G** is to revolutionize how we interact with the digital world, with promises of **ultra-high speeds**, **extremely low latency**, and **unprecedented connectivity**.

1. The Vision of 6G: What Will it Look Like?

While **5G** brought substantial improvements in terms of speed and connectivity, **6G** will take these concepts to new extremes, enabling **global connectivity** at an **exponential scale**. Think of it as the next evolutionary step that not only enhances our existing infrastructure but completely transforms how we interact with the world around us.

1.1 Key Features of 6G

1. **Speed and Data Transfer**:
   - **6G networks** are expected to achieve data speeds of up to **100 Gbps**, compared to **5G's maximum of 10 Gbps**. This will allow for **ultra-high-definition video, real-time holographic communication**, and seamless **remote collaboration** in **virtual environments**.
2. **Extremely Low Latency**:
   - **6G** promises to reduce **latency** to nearly **zero** (as low as **0.1 milliseconds**). This ultra-low latency will be crucial for applications like **autonomous vehicles, remote surgery**, and other **mission-critical operations** where every millisecond counts.
3. **Massive Device Connectivity**:
   - **6G networks** will be designed to support the simultaneous connection of **trillions of devices**. From **wearables** and **smart homes** to **IoT devices** in cities, everything will be connected, communicating in real-time, and functioning as part of a **smart ecosystem**.
4. **AI-Integrated Networks**:
   - **Artificial Intelligence (AI)** and **machine learning (ML)** will become deeply integrated into **6G networks**, enabling them to be **self-organizing, self-healing**, and **predictive**. This means that the network will automatically optimize itself based on demand, **traffic patterns**, and even anticipate potential failures before they happen.

1.2 What Makes 6G Unique?

While **5G** primarily focused on **speed** and **low latency**, **6G** will provide **ubiquitous connectivity**—a truly **global network** that not only connects users but connects **devices, machines**, and even **virtual environments**. The vision is a **completely integrated** and **intelligent digital ecosystem**, with technologies like **holographic communications, quantum computing**, and **AI-driven automation** playing key roles.

2. The Road to 6G: Key Technologies and Advancements

The development of **6G** will involve overcoming significant technical challenges. New technologies, improved hardware, and network architectures will need to be integrated to meet the demands of the **6G era**.

2.1 Terahertz Spectrum

- **Terahertz (THz)** waves, which sit between **microwave** and **infrared** frequencies, are expected to be a cornerstone of **6G**. These waves can support the **extremely high data rates** that will be needed for **6G** applications such as **holographic communication** and **real-time AI processing**.
- The **terahertz spectrum** will allow **6G networks** to deliver **multi-gigabit** speeds, handling large volumes of data with minimal interference. However, **THz frequencies** have limitations in terms of **range** and **penetration**, which means advanced **network designs** will be necessary to ensure reliable connections.

Practical Insight:
Nokia and **Samsung** are already conducting research on **terahertz communication**, testing new materials and designs to make **THz frequencies** usable for next-gen wireless communication.

2.2 Advanced AI and Machine Learning

- **6G networks** will be inherently **AI-driven**. With the ability to **self-manage** and **self-optimize**, these networks will rely on **advanced machine learning** to make real-time decisions based on network conditions, user demands, and environmental factors. AI will also play a role in **predictive maintenance**, identifying potential failures before they disrupt the network.
- **AI-driven automation** will also enhance the **intelligence** of **smart cities**, **autonomous vehicles**, and **smart homes**. The **AI algorithms** embedded in **6G networks** will process **massive amounts of data** from **IoT devices** in real-time, enabling faster decision-making across industries.

Practical Example:
In **smart cities**, **6G** could use AI to manage everything from **traffic flow** to **energy usage**. For instance, AI could adjust **traffic lights** dynamically based on real-time data, reducing congestion and optimizing travel times.

2.3 Quantum Computing

- **Quantum computing** will play an important role in **6G networks**, potentially revolutionizing how data is processed and transmitted. Quantum computing can handle complex problems exponentially faster than classical computing, making it ideal for applications that require high-speed processing, such as **AI**, **machine learning**, and **data encryption**.
- **Quantum encryption** will also enhance the **security** of **6G networks**, ensuring that communication is tamper-proof and secure from quantum threats.

Practical Example:
Google and **IBM** are already at the forefront of **quantum computing** development. Their advancements in quantum technology could eventually lead to more secure **6G networks**, offering encryption techniques that are **impossible to crack** with classical computing methods.

---

3. The Role of 5G in Laying the Foundation for 6G

Although **6G** is still years away, **5G technology** is laying the groundwork for its eventual deployment. **5G** networks are already providing **speed**, **connectivity**, and **low latency**, which are essential for the future development of **6G**. The real-time data processing and **AI integration** enabled by **5G** are building blocks that **6G** will improve upon.

3.1 Massive Device Connectivity: Scaling Up the IoT

- **5G** has already begun connecting billions of devices, and **6G** will further scale this up to connect trillions of devices, creating a **hyper-connected world**. From **wearables** to **autonomous systems**, **5G's low latency** and **high bandwidth** provide the foundation for the next-generation **IoT** systems that will thrive in **6G**.
- The **Internet of Everything** (IoE), a vision in which every **device**, **machine**, and **sensor** is interconnected, will become a reality with **6G**. **5G** will make it possible to manage the vast number of devices and data points that will be present in **6G**, which will support the

infrastructure needed for **intelligent cities, connected vehicles,** and **smart environments**.

Practical Example:
In **smart manufacturing, 5G** enables real-time monitoring of equipment, machinery, and environmental conditions. As **6G** develops, this system will scale to accommodate even more **sensors, devices,** and **AI algorithms**, creating an **autonomous production ecosystem** where everything from inventory management to maintenance is automated.

3.2 Autonomous Systems and AI-Powered Automation

- **5G networks** are enabling the development of **autonomous systems** such as **self-driving cars** and **drones**. These systems rely on **real-time communication** to function effectively, and **5G**'s **low latency** and **high-speed data transfer** are essential for their operation.
- As **5G** accelerates the deployment of **autonomous vehicles** and **AI-powered systems, 6G** will enhance their capabilities, enabling them to **self-optimize** and make **intelligent decisions** based on massive amounts of real-time data. **6G** will improve the coordination of autonomous systems in dynamic environments, enabling safer, more efficient operations across industries.

---

4. Challenges on the Road to 6G

While the potential of **6G** is exciting, there are significant challenges to overcome.

4.1 Spectrum Limitations and THz Communication

- **Terahertz frequencies** are essential for **6G**, but using them for communication presents challenges such as **signal attenuation, power requirements,** and **limited range**. Researchers are working on new materials and technologies to address these limitations and make **THz communication** feasible at scale.

4.2 Security and Privacy

- With the **vast expansion of connected devices** and the integration of **AI** and **quantum computing**, ensuring the security and privacy of **6G networks** will be a major concern. Advanced **encryption techniques** and **AI-driven cybersecurity** solutions will be required to protect against both **traditional threats** and new **quantum-based attacks**.

4.3 Infrastructure and Energy Demands

- **6G networks** will require extensive infrastructure, including **advanced antennas**, **terahertz transmitters**, and **edge computing nodes**. The energy demands of these systems could be significant, and new methods of **energy-efficient network design** will be needed to keep costs and environmental impact under control.

The Future Is Hyperconnected

The road to **6G** is paved with challenges, but the potential benefits are enormous. **6G** will revolutionize our world by creating a **hyperconnected digital ecosystem** where everything from **autonomous vehicles** to **smart cities** and **AI-driven networks** operates in seamless harmony. As **5G** continues to lay the foundation, future technologies such as **terahertz communication**, **quantum computing**, and **AI integration** will drive the next wave of innovation.

13.2 How 5G Paves the Way for Artificial Intelligence and IoT

The advent of **5G technology** is one of the most transformative forces driving the next generation of **Artificial Intelligence (AI)** and the **Internet of Things (IoT)**. As **5G networks** roll out globally, they are not just enabling faster internet speeds; they are unlocking new possibilities for **AI-driven automation**, **intelligent devices**, and a **hyperconnected world**. **5G** creates the ideal environment for **AI** and **IoT** to thrive, enabling real-time, **massive-scale** data exchange and **low-latency** communication.

---

1. 5G and the Internet of Things (IoT): A Perfect Match

The **Internet of Things (IoT)** refers to the network of **smart devices** that collect, share, and exchange data over the internet. These devices range from **wearables** and **smart thermostats** to **industrial machines** and **connected cars**. **5G** enhances the **IoT ecosystem** by providing faster, more reliable connections for billions of devices that need to communicate in real time.

1.1 How 5G Powers IoT Devices

- **Massive Device Connectivity**: **5G networks** are designed to handle **massive numbers of connected devices** simultaneously. While **4G** networks struggle to support dense, high-volume connections, **5G** can support up to **1 million devices per square kilometer**. This makes **5G** the perfect infrastructure for the **growing IoT ecosystem**.
- **Low Latency for Real-Time Communication**: Many **IoT applications**—especially those in industries like **healthcare**, **automotive**, and **manufacturing**—require **real-time communication** between devices and systems. **5G's ultra-low latency** (as low as **1 millisecond**) allows **IoT devices** to send and receive data almost instantaneously, ensuring that actions are taken in real time. For example, a **smart car** can communicate with **traffic lights** and **other vehicles** to make decisions about speed, route, or stopping, all in real time.
- **High-Speed Data Transfer**: **5G's high data transfer rates** enable **IoT devices** to exchange **large volumes of data** with minimal delay. For instance, devices like **smart cameras** and **wearable health monitors** can stream high-definition data continuously without lag, allowing for **better performance** and **enhanced capabilities**.

Practical Example:
In **smart cities**, **5G-powered IoT** is being used to create **intelligent traffic management systems**. **IoT devices**, such as **smart traffic lights**,

sensors, and **cameras**, send real-time data to a central system that can adjust traffic flows based on live conditions. **5G** ensures this data is transmitted **instantly**, reducing congestion, improving safety, and enhancing efficiency.

1.2 Real-Time Data Processing and Automation

- **Edge Computing**: **5G** enables **edge computing**, which processes data closer to the source (i.e., at the device level or near the network edge), rather than sending everything to a centralized cloud server. This reduces latency and ensures that **IoT devices** can make **real-time decisions**. For example, **self-driving cars** use **edge computing** to process data from **sensors**, allowing the car to make split-second decisions about braking, steering, or avoiding obstacles.
- **Data-Driven Automation**: With **5G**, IoT devices can operate autonomously based on data inputs from the environment. This is critical for **smart homes** where **automated lighting**, **security systems**, and **temperature controls** respond to real-time data from devices and sensors, optimizing comfort and energy efficiency.

Practical Example:
In **smart factories**, **IoT sensors** on machines monitor real-time performance data such as **temperature**, **pressure**, and **vibration**. With **5G**, this data is processed in real-time, enabling **predictive maintenance**. If a sensor detects an anomaly, it can trigger automated repairs, preventing equipment failure and reducing downtime.

---

2. 5G and Artificial Intelligence (AI): Driving Smarter Systems

AI refers to the ability of machines to **learn**, **adapt**, and **make decisions** based on data. **5G networks** are the perfect platform for **AI** because they provide the **speed**, **reliability**, and **scalability** needed to process large volumes of data quickly and efficiently.

2.1 Real-Time AI Processing with 5G

- **Data-Intensive AI Models**: AI applications often require large datasets to train models and make decisions. **5G's high-speed data transfer** enables **real-time processing** of **big data**, facilitating faster **machine learning** and **deep learning** processes. This is especially important for applications like **predictive analytics** and **autonomous vehicles**, where quick decision-making is crucial.
- **AI-Powered Automation**: 5G allows **AI models** to operate at the **edge of the network**—where data is collected—so that decisions can be made **immediately**. For example, **AI systems** in **smart homes** can use **5G-powered sensors** to adjust lighting, temperature, and security systems based on real-time inputs from the environment. Similarly, **AI-powered robots** in manufacturing plants can adjust their movements in real time based on feedback from **vision systems** and **sensors**, which are connected via **5G**.

Practical Example:
Google's Waymo self-driving cars rely on **5G networks** to enable **real-time AI processing**. As the car collects data from **radar**, **cameras**, and **lidar**, **AI algorithms** analyze this information instantly, helping the car make driving decisions without human intervention. **5G** ensures this data is processed quickly enough to allow for safe and efficient driving.

2.2 AI-Driven Network Management

5G networks will be **AI-powered** themselves. With **AI algorithms** managing network traffic, **5G networks** will become more **efficient** and **adaptive**, allowing them to respond dynamically to changes in user demand, environmental conditions, and network congestion.

- **Self-Optimizing Networks**: AI-driven systems will enable **5G networks** to automatically adjust bandwidth, signal strength, and connectivity protocols in real-time. This will ensure that users and devices have optimal connectivity, even in crowded environments like stadiums, airports, and urban centers.
- **AI-Enhanced Data Routing**: 5G networks will also use **AI algorithms** to route data more effectively. By predicting traffic patterns and **network congestion**, the system can prioritize certain types of data—such as **emergency services communications** or **real-time video streaming**—while optimizing the rest.

Practical Example:
Ericsson is working on **AI-driven network management** systems that optimize 5G connectivity in real-time. The **AI system** can prioritize certain applications (e.g., autonomous vehicles) and dynamically adjust network parameters based on **user demand** and **data traffic conditions**, ensuring high-quality service.

---

3. How 5G Enables IoT and AI to Transform Industries

The convergence of **5G**, **IoT**, and **AI** is already transforming industries across the globe. Let's look at specific examples of how this technology is being used to enhance **productivity**, **efficiency**, and **innovation**.

3.1 Healthcare: Real-Time Monitoring and Telemedicine

- **Remote Surgery**: **5G's low latency** and high-speed data transfer enable **real-time communication** between doctors and robotic surgical systems, enabling **remote surgery**. Surgeons can operate on patients located far away, making surgery accessible to people in remote areas.
- **Wearable Health Devices**: **5G-enabled IoT** devices, such as **smartwatches** and **fitness trackers**, can continuously monitor vital signs like **heart rate** and **blood oxygen levels**. This data can be transmitted to healthcare providers in **real-time** for analysis, helping doctors make timely decisions about patient care.
- **AI in Diagnostics**: **AI models** powered by **5G** can process real-time data from medical devices, imaging systems, and sensors to assist in **diagnosing** diseases. For instance, **AI algorithms** can analyze **X-rays** or **CT scans** for signs of conditions like **cancer** or **fractures**, offering faster diagnosis.

Practical Example:
In **China**, **5G-powered telemedicine** services are enabling doctors to provide remote consultations in real-time. The **AI system** analyzes patient data, such as **medical images**, and offers suggestions for treatment, which doctors review during the consultation.

3.2 Manufacturing: Smart Factories and Predictive Maintenance

- **Smart Manufacturing**: In **smart factories, 5G-enabled IoT** devices monitor the **performance** of machines and equipment in real time. This data is sent to an **AI-powered system** that automatically adjusts production schedules, detects issues, and prevents equipment breakdowns.
- **Predictive Maintenance**: With **5G**, manufacturers can use **real-time data** from machines to predict failures before they happen. AI algorithms analyze the data for patterns, and when an issue is detected, the system can schedule maintenance proactively, reducing downtime and maintenance costs.

Practical Example:
Siemens' smart factories use **5G-connected sensors** and **AI algorithms** to manage production lines in real-time. The sensors monitor machine health, and AI analyzes the data to predict when a machine might fail. Maintenance is scheduled based on this analysis, preventing unexpected downtime and optimizing factory performance.

3.3 Transportation: Autonomous Vehicles and Logistics

- **Autonomous Vehicles**: **AI-powered self-driving cars** rely on **5G** to communicate with infrastructure (traffic lights, other vehicles) in real-time. **AI algorithms** process data from **cameras** and **sensors** to make driving decisions, while **5G networks** ensure that information is transmitted almost instantaneously for safe operation.
- **Logistics**: **AI** is transforming **logistics** by using **real-time data** from **IoT-enabled trucks, smart warehouses,** and **drones**. **5G networks** allow these devices to exchange data quickly, enabling **AI systems** to optimize routes, predict delays, and ensure timely deliveries.

Practical Example:
Waymo, Google's self-driving car project, relies on **5G** to process data from **lidar, radar**, and **camera sensors**. **AI algorithms** analyze the data to navigate traffic, avoid obstacles, and ensure passenger safety. **5G's real-time communication** makes this process efficient and safe.

A Smarter, More Connected Future

5G is not just about faster speeds; it is the key enabler for the **AI-driven world** we are heading toward. The **convergence of 5G**, **IoT**, and **AI is** already transforming industries by making systems smarter, more efficient, and more automated. From **healthcare** to **manufacturing** and **transportation**, these technologies are driving the next phase of innovation, opening up new opportunities for **productivity**, **sustainability**, and **growth**.

13.3 Global Impact: Shaping Economies and Digital Societies

As **5G technology** continues to roll out globally, its transformative effects are rippling through economies, industries, and societies. Beyond the technical advancements it brings, **5G** has the power to reshape how we interact with the world, drive economic growth, and improve the quality of life for people worldwide. From enabling new business models to creating **digital societies**, **5G** is laying the groundwork for a **connected future** that will redefine the global landscape.

1. Economic Opportunities: Driving Growth and Innovation

1.1 Economic Growth through Digital Transformation

The introduction of **5G** networks is expected to significantly boost global **economic growth** by **enabling new technologies**, improving **productivity**, and creating **new markets**. According to a report from **IHS Markit**, **5G** could add **$13.2 trillion** to the global economy by 2035. This growth will come from sectors that can now leverage **high-speed, low-latency networks** to develop innovative products and services.

- **New Business Models**: 5G enables the creation of **new business models** that rely on real-time data exchange and intelligent decision-making. For example, **cloud gaming** services like **Google Stadia** and **Microsoft xCloud** rely on **5G's low latency** and **high-**

speed connectivity to deliver immersive gaming experiences to users without the need for powerful hardware. Similarly, **5G** is enabling the rise of **autonomous vehicles**, **smart factories**, and **AI-powered healthcare**, all of which will drive growth in their respective industries.

- **Enhancing Productivity**: **5G networks** are accelerating the **digital transformation** of traditional industries, allowing them to enhance their operations through **automation** and **real-time data analysis**. For example, **5G-powered IoT devices** in manufacturing can help companies track machine performance, predict failures, and optimize production processes, resulting in increased **efficiency** and **productivity**.

Practical Example:
China is investing heavily in **5G infrastructure**, with the goal of turning the country into a **global leader** in **smart manufacturing** and **digital innovation**. **5G** has already enabled companies like **Huawei** and **BYD** to enhance their manufacturing capabilities, create **smart factories**, and drive new **business models** that rely on **automation** and **AI**.

1.2 Job Creation and Economic Diversification

The rollout of **5G** also presents new opportunities for **job creation** and **economic diversification**. **5G** requires an extensive ecosystem of **infrastructure development**, including the construction of **base stations**, **small cells**, and the integration of **5G networks** into existing systems.

- **Construction and Network Deployment**: As **5G networks** are deployed, there will be a surge in demand for workers involved in **network infrastructure** and **construction**. This includes engineers, network technicians, and **telecom specialists** who will install and maintain **5G equipment**.
- **New Industries and Jobs**: The **5G-enabled economy** will lead to the creation of entirely new sectors and job types. For example, **5G-enabled smart factories** require new roles in **automation**, **robotics**, and **AI-powered systems**. Similarly, industries like **autonomous vehicles**, **telemedicine**, and **cloud gaming** will require new technical expertise and support staff.

Practical Example:
In **South Korea**, **5G networks** are expected to generate thousands of new

jobs in sectors ranging from **autonomous driving** to **smart healthcare**. The government has implemented training programs to prepare the workforce for these **new opportunities**, focusing on skills such as **AI development**, **5G network management**, and **IoT integration**.

2. Building Digital Societies: Smart Cities and Connected Communities

2.1 Smart Cities: The Backbone of Future Urbanization

The potential for **5G technology** to create **smart cities** is immense. By integrating **sensors**, **IoT devices**, and **advanced data analytics**, **5G** enables cities to become more **efficient**, **sustainable**, and **livable**. This will result in improved **urban management**, enhanced **quality of life**, and better **resource allocation**.

- **Urban Mobility**: **5G-enabled smart cities** can optimize traffic management through **real-time data** from **sensors** and **traffic lights**, reducing congestion and improving transportation efficiency. In **smart transportation**, **autonomous vehicles** can communicate with **infrastructure** and **other vehicles**, allowing for safer, more efficient travel.
- **Smart Infrastructure**: In **5G-connected smart cities**, infrastructure such as **streetlights**, **water systems**, and **energy grids** can be monitored and controlled remotely. This allows for real-time adjustments based on demand and environmental conditions, reducing waste and energy consumption. For instance, **smart streetlights** can automatically adjust brightness based on **pedestrian movement** or the time of day, saving energy and increasing safety.

Practical Example:
In **Barcelona**, the city has integrated **5G-powered IoT systems** to monitor everything from **traffic** to **waste management**. **Sensors** embedded in **waste bins** alert authorities when they're full, reducing unnecessary waste collection trips. Meanwhile, **5G-enabled smart parking systems** help drivers find available parking spots in real-time, reducing congestion and air pollution.

2.2 Digital Inclusion: Bridging the Connectivity Gap

5G networks also play a critical role in **digital inclusion**, helping bridge the **connectivity gap** between **urban** and **rural** areas. As **5G networks** expand, **remote areas** will gain access to high-speed internet, enabling **better access to healthcare, education, and economic opportunities**.

- **Remote Healthcare: Telemedicine** powered by **5G** allows individuals in rural areas to access healthcare services without the need to travel long distances. Real-time video consultations, remote diagnostics, and AI-powered health monitoring are just a few examples of how **5G** will enable **better healthcare access** in underserved regions.
- **Education**: **5G networks** will also help address the **education divide** by enabling **high-speed internet access** in remote schools. Students can participate in **virtual classrooms**, access **educational resources**, and even engage in **online exams** without worrying about slow or unreliable connections.

Practical Example:
In **India**, **5G-powered telemedicine services** are being deployed in rural areas to provide remote consultations. In **rural education programs**, **5G** allows **interactive learning** using **virtual classrooms**, providing a rich, immersive experience for students who would otherwise be limited by poor internet connectivity.

---

3. The Social and Ethical Implications of a Hyperconnected World

While **5G** promises many benefits, it also presents **social** and **ethical challenges** that need to be addressed as we transition into an **increasingly connected world**.

3.1 Privacy and Data Security Concerns

As **5G** enables **massive data collection** through **IoT devices** and **AI-driven networks**, concerns about **data privacy** and **security** will rise. **5G networks** will enable real-time surveillance, personalized data collection, and the monitoring of **individual behaviors**, raising questions about how this data is protected and used.

- **Regulation and Governance**: Governments and regulatory bodies will need to develop frameworks to ensure that **personal data** is protected and that **AI systems** are used ethically. This includes enforcing policies related to **data ownership**, **consent**, and **security**.
- **Cybersecurity**: As more devices and systems become connected, the **cybersecurity risks** also increase. Securing **5G networks** from **malicious attacks**, such as **hacking** and **data breaches**, will be critical to maintaining the trust and safety of users.

Practical Example:
The **European Union** has taken steps to address these challenges with the **General Data Protection Regulation (GDPR)**, which sets standards for **data protection** and **privacy** across all sectors. As **5G networks** expand, similar regulations may be needed to ensure **ethical AI** deployment and **secure data exchange** in smart cities and other 5G-enabled services.

3.2 The Digital Divide: Accessibility and Affordability

While **5G networks** have the potential to **improve digital inclusion**, they also risk exacerbating the **digital divide** if access to **5G technology** is not equitable.

- **Affordability**: The cost of **5G devices** and services could become a barrier for certain demographics, particularly in **developing countries** or **low-income areas**. If **5G networks** are expensive or inaccessible to a large portion of the population, it could lead to **increased inequality** in access to essential services like **education**, **healthcare**, and **employment**.
- **Access in Rural Areas**: While **5G networks** will help connect rural areas, the cost of **infrastructure development** and **maintenance** in sparsely populated regions may present a challenge. Governments and private companies will need to collaborate to ensure that **rural communities** are not left behind in the **5G revolution**.

Practical Example:
In **South Africa**, **5G networks** are being rolled out in **urban areas** first,

but initiatives are being developed to expand to **rural communities** as well. The government is working with private firms to reduce the costs of **5G infrastructure** in remote areas, ensuring that **5G** becomes accessible to a broader portion of the population.

A Hyperconnected World Powered by 5G

The global impact of **5G** is already being felt across economies, industries, and societies. From **economic growth** and **job creation** to the development of **smart cities** and **digital societies**, **5G** is laying the foundation for a future where **everything is connected**. While there are challenges to overcome—such as **privacy concerns, cybersecurity threats**, and **affordability issues**—the opportunities presented by **5G** are immense.

Conclusion: 5G's Transformative Power: Unlocking a Connected Future

The launch of **5G technology** represents a pivotal moment in the evolution of global connectivity. It's not just a new **network standard**; it's a **game changer** that is transforming how we live, work, and interact with the world around us. From **faster internet speeds** and **lower latency** to the ability to support billions of connected devices, **5G** is the catalyst for a range of innovations across industries and society at large.

In this conclusion, we'll recap the key insights covered throughout this book, explore how you can leverage **5G** for both **personal** and **professional growth**, and take a look at what the future holds for **connectivity** and **smart technologies**.

Recap of Key Insights

Throughout this book, we've explored how **5G** is revolutionizing **connectivity** and enabling **smart technologies** to flourish in nearly every sector. Here are the key takeaways:

1. **Speed and Latency**:
   5G is about more than just **faster speeds**. It delivers **blazing fast internet**, with speeds up to **10 times** faster than **4G**. The true power of **5G** lies in its **low latency**—the delay in data transfer is almost negligible, making real-time communication and instant decisions possible.
2. **Massive Device Connectivity**:
   One of the defining characteristics of **5G** is its ability to connect **millions of devices** simultaneously without compromising performance. This is essential for the **Internet of Things (IoT)**, enabling everything from **smart homes** to **connected factories** and **smart cities** to operate seamlessly.

3. **AI and Automation**:
   5G and **AI** are working hand-in-hand to power **smart automation systems**. Whether it's for **autonomous vehicles, manufacturing**, or **remote healthcare**, the combination of **5G's fast data transfer** and **AI's decision-making capabilities** is unlocking new levels of **efficiency** and **intelligence** across industries.
4. **The Road to 6G and Beyond**:
   As we look to the future, **6G** and other technologies will build on the foundation set by **5G**. The promise of **100 times faster speeds, zero latency**, and the integration of **quantum computing** will make **5G** seem like a stepping stone to the future.
5. **Global Impact and Smart Cities**:
   From **smart cities** to **connected healthcare** and **autonomous transport, 5G** is the backbone of **digital societies**. It is empowering industries, governments, and individuals to create **more efficient, sustainable**, and **inclusive** environments.

How to Leverage 5G for Personal and Professional Growth

The arrival of **5G** offers exciting new opportunities for both **personal** and **professional growth**. As this technology becomes ubiquitous, it's important to understand how you can harness it to stay ahead of the curve.

1. Embrace Smart Technologies in Daily Life

- **Smart Homes**: With **5G** enabling faster communication between devices, you can set up a **smart home** that connects everything from your **lights** and **thermostats** to your **security cameras** and **voice assistants**. The added benefit of **5G** means no lag time when you adjust settings or check in on your home remotely.
- **Wearables and Health**: If you're into health and fitness, **5G** can empower **wearables** like **smartwatches** and **fitness trackers** to collect and transmit real-time data. You can get **instant insights** on your health, from your **heart rate** to your **sleep patterns**, helping you make informed decisions about your well-being.

2. Upgrade Your Professional Toolkit

- **Remote Work**: With **5G**'s ability to support **high-definition video calls** and seamless **cloud collaboration**, remote work has become more effective than ever. Whether you're **telecommuting** or collaborating with colleagues across the world, **5G** ensures you have the tools for efficient, real-time communication and project management.
- **Learning and Development**: The **faster speeds** and **low latency** of **5G** will make learning through **virtual classrooms** and **online training** more interactive and engaging. **AR** and **VR** technologies, which are enabled by **5G**, will make **hands-on training** and **immersive learning experiences** more accessible than ever.

3. Position Yourself as a Future Leader

- **IoT Integration**: The future of business involves **IoT-driven innovation**, where devices and systems communicate with each other. Learn how **5G-powered IoT** can enhance everything from **supply chains** to **inventory management**, and consider how you might implement these solutions in your own industry to improve efficiency and reduce costs.
- **AI and Automation**: **5G** is the enabler of **AI-driven automation**. As an individual or business owner, being knowledgeable about how AI and automation can enhance your operations will be crucial. Keep an eye on emerging AI technologies that rely on **5G** to streamline processes like customer service (e.g., **chatbots**), predictive maintenance, and supply chain management.

Practical Insight:
To stay ahead professionally, consider taking courses on **5G technology**, **IoT integration**, and **AI development**. By understanding how **5G** connects with these disruptive technologies, you'll be better equipped to leverage their potential in your career.

What the Future Holds for Connectivity and Smart Technologies

Looking ahead, the future of **connectivity** is deeply intertwined with the rise of **smart technologies** and the increasing reliance on data-driven insights. Here's a glimpse of what's in store:

1. Seamless Connectivity with 6G and Beyond

While **5G** is already revolutionizing the digital world, **6G** will further expand on its capabilities, offering **exponentially faster speeds, zero latency**, and the ability to **integrate quantum computing** into networks. This will open up even more exciting possibilities, such as **holographic communications**, **AI-powered decision-making** at an unprecedented scale, and **real-time global collaboration** without any noticeable delay.

2. Ubiquitous Smart Cities

Smart cities powered by **5G** will become more **interconnected**, with **real-time monitoring systems** and **autonomous operations** making urban life more efficient and sustainable. From **energy-efficient buildings** to **intelligent transportation** and **automated waste management**, the potential to create **cities that think** is becoming more tangible.

3. Hyper-Personalized Experiences

With **5G** enabling the seamless integration of **IoT** and **AI**, **consumer experiences** will become increasingly **personalized**. Think of **customized shopping experiences** where your **smart devices** know your preferences and automatically suggest products, or **virtual assistants** that predict your needs and offer solutions in real-time. The idea of a **truly smart world**—where everything from **healthcare** to **shopping** is tailored to your preferences—will be powered by **5G**.

Embracing the Future of Connectivity

As we conclude this journey through the **5G revolution**, it's clear that **5G** is not just about **faster speeds** and **better connectivity**; it's about fundamentally changing how we live, work, and interact with the world around us. From **smart homes** and **connected cities** to **AI-powered innovation** and **digital economies**, **5G** is laying the foundation for a **more connected, efficient, and intelligent future**.

For **personal growth**, it's about embracing new technologies, staying ahead of the curve with **AI** and **IoT**, and leveraging **5G's power** to create smarter and more efficient daily lives. For **professional growth**, it's about understanding how these technologies can transform industries, enhancing **productivity**, **creativity**, and **sustainability**.

Looking forward, the evolution of **5G** will continue with **6G** and beyond, creating new opportunities for innovation and **disrupting industries** on a global scale. Whether you are a **business leader**, a **tech enthusiast**, or simply someone looking to understand the future, the key is to stay connected, stay informed, and embrace the possibilities of this hyperconnected world.

Appendices

In this section, we'll provide useful supplementary information to help deepen your understanding of **5G technology** and its broader context. From a glossary of key terms to resources for further exploration, and an overview of the key standards and organizations shaping the future of **5G**, this section will serve as a valuable reference guide as you continue to explore the world of **connectivity** and **smart technologies**.

Glossary of Key 5G Terms

A clear understanding of the terminology surrounding **5G** is essential for navigating this rapidly evolving field. Here's a list of some of the most commonly used terms and their definitions:

- **5G**: The fifth generation of wireless technology, offering significantly faster speeds, lower latency, and higher connectivity than previous generations like **4G**.
- **Latency**: The time it takes for data to travel from the source to the destination. **5G** offers ultra-low latency, often as low as **1 millisecond**, enabling real-time communication.
- **Bandwidth**: The amount of data that can be transferred over a network in a given amount of time. **5G** offers much higher bandwidth than **4G**, supporting faster data transfer.
- **Millimeter Wave (mmWave)**: A high-frequency band of spectrum used by **5G** networks. It offers very high data speeds but has limited range and can be blocked by physical obstacles.
- **Small Cells**: Small, low-powered cellular radio access nodes that help increase network coverage and capacity, especially in dense urban areas.
- **Network Slicing**: A feature of **5G** that allows operators to create multiple virtual networks, each tailored to specific use cases or services, such as healthcare, autonomous vehicles, or entertainment.
- **Massive MIMO**: Short for **Massive Multiple Input Multiple Output**, this technology uses a large number of antennas to improve data throughput and signal quality, especially in high-traffic areas.

- **Edge Computing**: A distributed computing framework that processes data closer to the source (i.e., at the "edge" of the network) to reduce latency and bandwidth use, essential for real-time processing.
- **IoT (Internet of Things)**: The network of interconnected devices, sensors, and objects that collect and share data. **5G** enables **IoT** to scale up significantly with low latency and high capacity.
- **Virtual Reality (VR)**: A simulated experience that can be similar to or completely different from the real world. **5G** enables higher-quality **VR** by reducing latency and increasing data throughput.
- **Autonomous Vehicles**: Vehicles that use sensors, AI, and communication systems to drive themselves without human intervention. **5G** plays a crucial role in providing the low latency required for real-time communication between vehicles and infrastructure.
- **TeraHertz Spectrum**: A higher-frequency spectrum that will likely be used by future generations of wireless networks, including **6G**. It offers extremely high data speeds and could support innovations like **holographic communication**.

Resources for Further Reading

If you're looking to dive deeper into **5G technology**, here's a selection of useful resources, ranging from books and articles to online platforms and courses. These will help you stay updated and expand your knowledge:

Books

1. **"The 5G Myth: When Vision Decoupled from Reality"** by William Webb
   - A critical examination of the **hype** and **realities** surrounding **5G** technology. It provides an insightful look at the promises and challenges of **5G** adoption.
2. **"5G Mobile Networks: A Systems Approach"** by Chris Johnson and Andrew L. J. Cooper
   - This book offers a comprehensive technical approach to understanding the architecture, protocols, and systems behind **5G networks**.
3. **"5G for Dummies"** by Bill Rojas and Lawrence Harte

- A beginner-friendly guide to **5G**, covering everything from the basics of mobile connectivity to how **5G** will change industries and society.

Online Platforms and Articles

1. **GSMA (GSM Association)**
   - Website: *https://www.gsma.com/*
   - GSMA is an industry body that represents the mobile network operators. Their **5G hub** provides valuable articles, reports, and insights on **5G** deployment and trends.
2. **IEEE (Institute of Electrical and Electronics Engineers) 5G**
   - Website: *https://5g.ieee.org/*
   - IEEE is one of the leading standards organizations in the world for **wireless technologies**. Their **5G portal** offers in-depth technical articles, white papers, and research on the future of mobile networks.
3. **5G Americas**
   - Website: *https://www.5gamericas.org/*
   - An industry trade association focused on the development and promotion of **5G** technologies. Their website features useful reports, webinars, and resources on **5G standards** and development.

Online Courses

1. **Coursera - "5G Technology" by Yonsei University**
   - Coursera offers a course on **5G technology** that covers the fundamentals of **5G networks**, its capabilities, and its application in different industries.
   - Website: *https://www.coursera.org/*
2. **edX - "5G for Everyone" by University of California, San Diego**
   - An introductory course that explains the technical and business aspects of **5G** and how it can transform various sectors.
   - Website*: https://www.edx.org/*
3. **LinkedIn Learning - "Understanding 5G"**
   - A more accessible introduction to **5G** technology, exploring how **5G** differs from previous generations, its applications, and its impact on society.

5G Industry Standards and Organizations

Several organizations play a critical role in defining the **standards** and **protocols** that guide the development and deployment of **5G networks** worldwide. Understanding these standards is key to staying informed about the direction of **5G technology**.

1. 3rd Generation Partnership Project (3GPP)

- Website: *https://www.3gpp.org/*
- **3GPP** is the main body responsible for developing the technical specifications for **5G** (and earlier generations). It brings together telecommunications organizations from around the world to standardize **mobile communications**.

2. International Telecommunication Union (ITU)

- Website: *https://www.itu.int/en/ITU-T/5G/*
- The **ITU** is a United Nations agency that coordinates global telecommunications. It plays a crucial role in defining **global standards** for **5G networks**, ensuring that they are interoperable across borders.

3. GSMA (Global System for Mobile Communications Association)

- Website: *https://www.gsma.com/*
- GSMA represents **mobile operators** and works to advance the interests of **mobile communications** worldwide. It's heavily involved in promoting **5G** adoption, **policy**, and **global standards**.

4. Open RAN Alliance

- Website: *https://www.openran.org/*
- The **Open RAN Alliance** is a group of companies that aim to make **5G infrastructure** more **open** and **interoperable**. They are focusing on reducing network costs and improving flexibility by

using **open interfaces** and **virtualized solutions** in **radio access networks (RAN)**.

5. Institute of Electrical and Electronics Engineers (IEEE)

- Website*: https://www.ieee.org/*
- **IEEE** is an influential standards organization that plays a role in developing **5G technologies**, particularly in **wireless communications** and **networking protocols**.

The journey through **5G technology** has opened our eyes to the vast potential of the **next-generation connectivity** that is about to change the world. With **5G** now being rolled out globally, understanding the **key terms**, staying up-to-date with the latest resources, and familiarizing yourself with the key **standards organizations** will help you stay ahead of the curve. Whether you're a **student**, a **professional**, or just an enthusiast, these resources will empower you to dive deeper into the **5G revolution** and fully harness its power.

As **5G** continues to evolve, staying informed will not only enhance your understanding of **smart technologies**, but also position you to leverage these advancements for personal and professional growth. The future of **5G** is bright, and it's just beginning!

www.ingramcontent.com/pod-product-compliance
Lightning Source LLC
LaVergne TN
LVHW081523050326
832903LV00025B/1596